THE WHISPERING OF GHOSTS

THE WHISPERING OF GHOSTS

Trauma and Resilience

Boris Cyrulnik

Translated by Susan Fairfield

Other Press • New York

Ouvrage publié avec le concours du Ministère français chargé de la culture–Centre National du Livre.

We wish to express our appreciation to the French Ministry of Culture for its assistance in the preparation of the translation.

Originally published as *Le murmure des fantômes*
Copyright © Editions Odile Jacob, January 2003

Translation copyright © 2005 Susan Fairfield

Production Editor: Robert D. Hack

Text design: Kaoru Tamura

This book was set in Fournier MT by Alpha Graphics of Pittsfield, NH.

10 9 8 7 6 5 4 3 2 1

Library of Congress Cataloging-in-Publication Data

Cyrulnik, Boris.
    [Murmure des fantômes. English]
    The whispering of ghosts : trauma and resilience / by Boris Cyrulnik ; translated from the French by Susan Fairfield.
        p. cm.
    Includes bibliographical references.
    ISBN 1-59051-114-X (hardcover : alk. paper) 1. Resilience (Personality trait) 2. Resilience (Personality trait)–Case studies. I. Title.
    BF698.35.R47C9713 2004
    155.2'4–dc22
                                                              2004003830

Contents

Introduction*

No one could guess that she was a ghost. She was too pretty for that, too sweet, radiant. A phantom doesn't have any warmth; it's a cold sheet, a piece of cloth, a disturbing shadow. But she delighted us. We should have been suspicious. What power did she have to charm us so, to take hold of us and carry us away for our greatest happiness? We were trapped to the point of not understanding that she had been dead for a long time.

Actually, Marilyn Monroe was not wholly dead, just a little, and at times a little more. By awakening a delicious feeling in us, her charm kept us from understanding that one doesn't have to be dead in order not to be alive. She had begun not to be alive at birth. Her mother, dreadfully unhappy and banished from the human race because she had brought an illegitimate little girl into the world, was numb with misery. A baby can develop only within the laws invented by mankind, and even before her birth, little Norma Jean Baker was already an outlaw. Her mother was so overcome by melancholy that she wasn't strong enough to offer her a safe

*Translator's note: An earlier version of the translation was done by Marjolijn de Jager.

embrace. The future Marilyn had to be placed in icy orphanages and entrusted to a succession of foster families in which it was hard to learn how to love.

Children without families count less. Exploiting them sexually or socially is not an especially major crime, because these little abandoned ones aren't fully real children. That's how some people think. In order to survive despite the abuse, little "Marilyn" had to start fantasizing, feeding on her very pain, before sinking into her mother's melancholia and madness.[1] And so she claimed that Clark Gable was her true father and that she belonged to a royal family. And why not? This is how she constituted a vague identity for herself, since without crazy dreams she would have had to live in a world of mud. When a traumatic reality is dead, delusion brings a surge of happiness. So she married a baseball star for whom she cooked peas and carrots every night because he liked the colors so much.

In Manhattan, where she took acting lessons, she became the favorite student of Lee Strasberg, who was fascinated by her odd grace. She needed a lot of stimulation to keep from succumbing to non-life. She would grow sluggish, refusing to leave her bed or to wash. When a kiss awakened her—the kiss of Arthur Miller, for whom she converted to Judaism, or John Kennedy's, or Yves Montand's—she would come back to life, dazzling and warm, and no one realized that this enchanting woman was a ghost. And yet she said so when she sang "I'm Through with Love," but, already in the back of beyond, radiant in all her glory, she knew that she had only three more years to live before giving herself one last gift: death.

Marilyn was never fully alive, but we couldn't know this because her marvelous ghost bewitched us so.

The last biography of Hans Christian Andersen begins with this sentence: "My life is a beautiful fairy tale, rich and happy."[2] We must always believe what authors write. In any event, the first line of a book is often fraught with meaning. When little Hans Christian came into the world in Denmark in 1805, his mother had been forced into prostitution by her own mother, who beat her and forced clients on her. Pregnant with Hans Christian, the girl had fled and married Mr. Andersen. This woman would do anything to keep her son from knowing poverty. She became a laundress, and the father enlisted in Napoleon's army. Alcoholic and illiterate, she died in an attack of delirium tremens, and the father killed himself in a fit of madness.

The little boy had to work in a textile mill, then in a tobacco factory where human relationships were often violent. Yet Hans Christian, born into the prostitution, madness, and the death of his parents, and living amid violence and destitution, never lacked affection. "Very ugly, sweet and nice as a girl," he first basked in his mother's wish to make him happy; then, in the loving home of his paternal grandmother, he was tenderly brought up with the help of a woman neighbor who taught him to read. The community of Odense on the green island of Fionia, with its five thousand inhabitants, had a strong tradition of storytelling. Poetry made a frequent appearance in the meetings where the Icelandic saga was recounted and the games of the Greenland Inuits were played. Craftsmanship, celebrations, and processions marked the life of this warm group, and it was good to be a part of it.

We can imagine that little Hans took notice of the world around him in his early years, a world in the form of what we might call an oxymoron: two antithetical terms come together in their opposition, just as the vaults of a roof are supported because they stand against each other. This odd combination of words allows us to talk, without contradiction, about a "dark brightness" or a "wonderful misfortune." Little Andersen's world was to be organized around these two forces. He absolutely had to tear himself away from the mire of his origins in order to live in his culture's emotional brightness and the strange beauty of its stories.

These contrary worlds were linked by the art that transforms mud into poetry, suffering into ecstasy, the ugly duckling into a swan. The oxymoron constituting the universe in which the child grew up was quickly incorporated into his personal memory. His mother, who warmed him with her tenderness, was drowning in alcohol and died in the vomit of DTs. One of his grandmothers, ready to prostitute her daughter, was the incarnation of the woman as witch, while the other personified the woman as good fairy who gives life and beckons toward happiness. Thus little Hans learned, early on, about the representation of a split female world that would later turn him into a man strongly attracted by women and terrified by them.

His childhood was made up of constant humiliations and very real suffering that, in one and the same impetus, were connected to the daily delights of affectionate encounters and cultural marvels. Not only did he manage to bear the horror of his origins, but it was perhaps the frightening ordeal of his early years that actually emphasized the tenderness of women and the beauty of stories.

The oxymoron structuring his world would also characterize his life and govern his relationships as an adult. In a life history all we ever have is one problem to solve, the one that gives meaning to our life and imposes a style on our relationships. The despair of the ugly duckling was colored by admiration for the big white swans and enlivened by the hope of swimming alongside them so as to protect other little ugly children.

This pair of opposite forces that gave him the energy to "come out of the swamp and reach the light of royal courts" also explains his painful love affairs. This wounded man saved from the muck by feminine attachment was attracted by every woman, but, because he made the bond to women into something holy and women themselves into goddesses enlivening his daydreams, his sexuality was inhibited. He dared to love only from afar. There is a price to be paid for becoming a swan, and his resilience,[3] which cost him his sexuality, drove him toward a solitude that he filled with literary creations.

Hans Christian Andersen was born into his mother's prostitution, his parents' madness and death, early orphanhood, domestic poverty, and social violence. How not to remain dead when you live like that? Two embers of resilience revived his soul: the attachment to a few women that mended the self-esteem of the damaged child, and a cultural context of strange tales in which the language of the swamps made gnomes arise out of the mist, along with goblins, fairies, witches, elves, warriors, gods, weapons, swaggerers, sirens, match sellers, and ugly ducklings devoted to the dead mother.

Bond and meaning[4]: these two words make resilience possible, and Marilyn Monroe never encountered them. Without ties and without a history, how could you become yourself? When little Norma Jean was placed in an orphanage, no one could have imagined that one day she would become the breathtaking Marilyn. Emotional deprivation had turned her into a plucked, trembling, shriveled little bird unable to open up to the world and to people. The constant changes of foster families had made it impossible for her to surround herself with the emotional stability a child needs in order to feel lovable. The result was that when she reached the age of sexuality she let herself be taken by anyone who was kind to her.

When men didn't take advantage of her sexually they exploited her financially. It was in the interest of Darryl Zanuck, the film producer, to see her as a birdbrain so that he could make a fortune hiring her out to other studios. And even those who sincerely loved her couldn't enter into her inner world to help her create a story that would have made sense of her disturbed childhood. Her lovers enjoyed being trapped by the splendid image of sweet Marilyn. Blinded by such great beauty, we could not see her enormous despair. She remained alone in the mud where, from time to time, we would throw her a diamond—until the day when she let herself go.

Little Hans, escaped from hell, regained his taste for life. He kept company with swans, wrote stories, and had laws passed for the protection of other little ugly ducklings. Inventing heroes with whom many wounded children have identified was the way he compensated for the renunciation of relationships with women.[5] His escape from hell cost him his sexuality, but no one claims that resilience is a recipe for happiness. It is a strategy for struggle against unhappiness that makes it possible to seize some pleasure in life despite the whispering of ghosts in the depths of our memory.

Part I

Tiny Tots, or the Age of Bonding

1. Without Surprise, Nothing Would Emerge
from Traumatic Reality

We can't speak of resilience unless there has been a trauma followed by the resumption of some kind of development, a mended rip. It is not a question of normal development, since the trauma inscribed in memory is part of the person's history from now on, like a ghost that accompanies him. Someone with a wounded soul will be able to resume a course of development that, from now on, will be affected by a forced entry into his earlier personality.

The problem is simple. All we need to do to make it complicated is pose the question clearly. To this effect, I shall ask:

- What is an event?
- What is this traumatic violence that rips the protective bubble around a person?
- How does a trauma become integrated into the memory?
- What is the nature of the scaffolding that must surround the person after the uproar to enable him to resume life despite the wounding and his memory of it?

There were two kids in state custody at a farm in Néoules, near Brignoles, an older boy of 14 and René, age 7. The boys slept outside in a wooden barn, while Cécile, the hunchbacked daughter of the family, was entitled to a bed with white sheets in a room. The farmer's wife was harsh: "Marguerite ruled with a firm hand," the boys reported. Since she had nothing to say to the boys, whenever she passed them she would hit out at them with a stick for no reason.

She often missed, but what is striking (so to speak) is that, when the boys received a blow, they never blamed the farmer's wife. On the contrary, they reproached themselves: "You heard her coming, after all"; "You could have gotten into a better position to protect yourself." This interpretation explains why the pain of a blow is not a trauma. The boys were often in pain and would rub their heads or arms, but when they thought about what had happened, when they discussed it with one another or pictured it to themselves, the reason they didn't suffer all over again is that the blow came from someone they didn't love. We don't resent the stone we bump up against. It hurts and that's all. But when the blow comes from someone with whom we have established an emotional relationship, after enduring it we suffer a second time when we think about it.

The boys were not surprised at this feeling. Rage at having been trapped and self-accusation were already signs of resilience, as though they had thought, "There was a slight possibility that we could get away. When we heard her coming, we could have escaped, but we wasted the chance." Taking responsibility made them feel in control of their fate: "Today I'm small, alone, and incredibly dirty, but one day you'll see that I can get myself into a situation where I'll never get hit anymore." And, since the farmer's wife often missed her target, René paradoxically developed a sense of triumph in his mind: "I can have mastery over what happens."

Béatrice's mother wanted to be a dancer. Her physical and mental attributes promised a fine career, but when she became pregnant a few months before a dance competition her baby took on the meaning of a persecutor for her: "It's all over with my dreams because of the baby." So she hated her little girl, and, when we loathe someone, we have to find reasons why, right? The mother beat her, explaining that it was for her own good, so that she would grow up to be a better person.

Even as she was being hit, Béatrice used to think, "Poor Mom, you don't know how to control yourself; you aren't a real grownup." And this condescension protected her from the suffering involved in thinking about the blows.

Béatrice suffered only once. Yet she had to be separated from her mother because of the extent of the abuse. Placed with a neighbor, Béatrice felt guilty about being a burden to her: "She'd be glad if I weren't here. She really is very good to take me in." So the child became morbidly nice. She walked to school in order to save the bus fare and buy a present for her aunt. She got up early in the morning to do the household chores in silence, so that when the woman got up she would be surprised to see an immaculate house. The neighbor, of course, got used to having a clean kitchen, and one day, when she found the floor still dirty from the previous night's meal, she insulted Béatrice and, in her aroused state of anger, hit the girl with a broom. The blow did not hurt, but by invalidating Béatrice's efforts it led to despair lasting several days, during which the girl kept on replaying the scene of being hit with the broom. Béatrice suffered twice.

For someone to have the feeling of an event, a reality must cause a surprise and a meaning that make the thing salient, conspicuous. Without surprise, nothing would emerge from reality. Without salience, nothing would come into awareness. If a piece of traumatic reality "didn't mean anything," it would not even create a memory. This is why we are normally not aware of our breathing or of our struggle against the pull of gravity. When we do decide to pay attention to such things, we do not register a memory of them because these facts don't mean anything in particular except if we fall ill. When a fact is not integrated into our history because it has no meaning, it is erased. Thus we can write all the facts of the day in a private diary, but almost none of them will create a memory.

2. When the Fall of a Dishrag Becomes Terrifying

Certain scenarios will turn into memories and become landmarks of our narrative identity, like a series of wordless stories.

A patient related the following episode: "I clearly recall that, after I passed my high-school exam, I and another candidate were having a martini at a bar counter. I remember my young schoolmate's suede jacket, his haircut, and his face. I remember the curved counter of the bistro and the waiter's head. I even remember saying, "Now that we've got the diploma, we're worth something." I remember the stunned expression of my pal, who surely thought he was worth something before he passed the exam."

In this way, the man telling this story had extracted this scenario from the jumble of reality, making it a brick in the construction of his identity. Because he was an abandoned child, a factory worker since the age of 12, passing the high-school exam took on the significance of an extraordinary event for him, one that would allow him to become an engineer. School meant "reparation," "compensation" for a teenager who, without the diploma, would have found it hard to feel that he mattered. The series of images arising from drinking a martini formed the ritual of a scenario that would become a signpost in his memory.

Without an event there is no self-representation. What illuminates a piece of reality so as to make it an event is the way in which the environment had made the person sensitive to this type of information.

We can speak of trauma only if the overwhelming—or sometimes sneaky—surprise floods the person, shakes him up, and carries him into a torrent in a direction he would not have wanted to go. At the moment when the event tears his protective bubble, disorganizes his world, and sometimes throws him into confusion, the person who is not fully aware of what is happening to him is at a loss and, like René, suffers blows. But we have to give meaning to the sudden disaster as soon as possible in order not to remain in this state of confusion in which we can't make any decisions because we don't understand anything. And so it is a representation—a re-presentation—of images and words that will once again be able to form a personal world by restoring clear vision.

Whereas the traumatic event imposes itself on us and brings our life into disarray, the meaning we assign to the event depends on our history and on the rituals in our environment. This is why Béatrice suffered when the neighbor hit her with a broom (which meant that her emotional strategy had failed), more than she suffered from her mother's serious abuse. Hence there is no such thing as an "event as such," since a piece of reality can take on special meaning in one context and be quite ordinary in another.

In a situation of sensory isolation, all perceptions are changed. When you go into the kitchen to get a glass of water, you may happen to see a dishrag without being devastated. But when you are alone in prison, separated from the world for several months, and you see the same rag, it becomes an event:

"I was dozing, my mind a blank, when I heard a noise behind me. The rag had just fallen from the railing, as lithe as a cat. It wasn't moving, but it seemed to me that any minute it was going to crouch and jump up. I looked up, and that's when I saw it. The shadow of the rag formed the silhouette of a hanged man on the wall. I couldn't keep my eyes off it. I spent a whole afternoon facing this ghost."[6] In a social context, a rag doesn't establish a memory, but in a context of sensory deprivation the frightening shadow it forms on the wall becomes a landmark in a person's life history.

This is how emotional restriction constitutes a major sensory privation, an insidious trauma that is all the more damaging because it's hard to become aware of it, to make it into an event, a memory that we could confront and rework. When we don't come face-to-face with a recollection, it haunts us, like a shadow in our inner world, and instead of our working on it, it works on us.

Sensory isolation, in itself, is an emotional privation. The isolated person is no longer affected by the same conspicuous objects, which explains the astonishing differences in the attachments of people who have been emotionally deprived. Affection is such a vital need that, when we don't get it, we become intensely attached to any event that brings back even a little bit of life to us, whatever the cost: "Being all alone is the worst suffering. You keep on wanting something to happen; you spend your time waiting for the 'grub,' for the walk, for bedtime, for someone to come. In the morning, you're sometimes quite happy to see the assistant, even if only for a few seconds. . . . Solitude produces odd effects."[7]

In such a situation, the smallest sign fills the void in a life. The deprived person, starving for sensory stimulation, hypersensitive to the slightest signal, notices an unexpected sigh, a tiny smile, a frown. In a normal sensory context, these signs do not take on meaning, but, in a world of emotional deprivation, they become a major event. "Above all, never make noise. Don't draw attention to your presence," said the psychiatrist Tony Lainé when he had to help David, a child who was shut up in a closet while his mother was traveling.[8]

No attachment had formed between this mother and the boy. Whenever she saw her son, she abused him terribly: "She'd make me kneel on an iron bar for hours with my nose against the wall. Or she'd lock me in the bathroom for days on end."[9] But one day, a Sunday, she came looking for him and—an amazing event—took him for a walk! All his life David would remember that radiant Sunday when she held his hand. (Who remembers Sundays when their mother held their hand? Certainly not those whose hand she held every day.)

David's emotional deprivation transformed an ordinary gesture into a notable adventure. No child who has been loved in the right way ever builds a memory on such an everyday emotional occurrence. This is not to say that he doesn't establish it in memory. Quite the contrary: the emotional ordinariness forms a sense of safety in his brain. And it is gaining this self-confidence that teaches him the gentle boldness of emotional conquests. Without knowing it, such a child has learned an easy way to love. But he will never be able to recall how this came about.

Some children who have been deprived of affection construct their narrative identity around these splendid moments when people were willing to love them. The result is astonishing biographies in which the child abandoned in an orphanage, left alone in a cellar, raped, beaten, and constantly humiliated becomes a resilient adult who can calmly say that he has always been lucky in life. From the depths of his quagmire and despair he was eager for the few shining moments when he received an emotional gift that he made into a memory revisited a thousand times: "One Sunday, she held my hand."

3. A Children's Round Dance as Magic Wand

When it isn't possible for us to work on our memories, the shadow of the past works on us. Deprived children, hypersensitive to the slightest emotional input, can make it into a magnificent event or a despondent one, depending on what they encounter in their environment.

Bruno had been abandoned because he was born out of wedlock, which, in Canada forty years ago, was considered a major crime. Left alone, the child had a "relationship" only with his hands, which he constantly kept in motion, and his own spinning in circles, both of which created a sense of event in him, a bit of life in spite of everything.

After several years of emotional isolation, he was placed in a residence that was warm enough to cause these symptoms to disappear. Yet he had retained a way of loving that seemed distant and cold but at least didn't frighten him. This adaptation, which made him feel secure, was not a resilience factor, since, even though it calmed the child, it prevented him from resuming his emotional development.

One evening a kindly nun had organized a round dance in which, when a boy asked a girl to dance, he had to sing:

> It's Rosine I prefer, for she's the prettier of the two.
> Ah, Ginette, if you think I love you,
> My little heart is not made for you.
> It is made for the one I love,
> Who is prettier than you.

When Bruno and another boy were invited by a girl to twirl around in the middle of the large circle formed by the other children, it was as though he were numbed by this unbelievable choice. But when he heard the whole circle of children singing in chorus: "It's Bruno I prefer," he no longer heard the rest of the song. His world had just exploded like a huge light, an immense joy, an expansion that gave him an amazing feeling of lightness. He twirled around like a madman with the little girl.

Then, forgetting to go back to the circle, he ran and hid under his bed, incredibly happy. He really could be loved!

The other little boy, somewhat disappointed, sulked for thirty seconds, time enough to realize that other children, like him, could not be the preferred ones. Then he forgot the whole thing. This little setback was never an event for him. Because he had been a loved child, the circle dance had no special meaning for him. For Bruno, on the other hand, it was a revelation, one he kept on thinking back to. Even today, forty years later, he smiles when he tells about this major event that changed the way he loved.

We are unconsciously shaped by the reality around us. The imprint of reality is etched in our memory without our realizing it, without becoming an event. We learn to love unbeknownst to ourselves, without even being aware of the way in which we love. Perhaps Freud had in mind this form of memory, active but without recollection, when he spoke of the biological rock of the unconscious.[10]

The event is an inauguration, like a birth into a self-representation.[11] For Bruno, there will always be a before and an after when it comes to the round dance. Lack of affection had made him famished, terrified by the intensity of his need. His unhappiness had left a biological trace in him, a sensitivity that made him take special notice of this type of event. If he had missed this round dance, he would have come upon a similar one later on. But if the cultural context had prohibited such dances or had organized society in such a way that illegitimate children did not have the right to dance, Bruno would have established these traces of emotional deprivation firmly in his memory. He would have learned them without knowing it, and his apparently icy, self-centered behavior would never have been able to be warmed by this kind of encounter. The event would never have taken place.

Today the scene of the round dance is a milestone in Bruno's narrative identity: "Something astounding happened to me. I was transformed by a dance." But a life cycle, a life as a whole, can't end after the first chapter. And so, looking back on his past, Bruno will seek out experiences that will enable him to pursue his transformation and work on it so as to shed light on the darkness of his early childhood: "I don't hold a grudge against my mother for abandoning me. That's what you had to do back then. She must have suffered a lot herself." The account of his past, its intentional refashioning, eases the shadow that was looming over him. The abandonment that had imbued him with his sad way of loving became, in his self-representation, a wound, a lack that he could rework with the passage of time. For certain events are metaphors of the self: "After that round dance, I understood how to make friends. I've been very lucky in life. When Sister Marie took me for IQ testing, she whispered the answers I was supposed to give. My scores were good, and I was put on the academic track. Today I'm a literature professor."

4. How People Make Things Speak

The archaeology of a crypt, the illumination of a shadowy area in our history, can even become a thrilling quest when a mystery is revealed and those around us take part in the exploration.

Every trauma shakes us up and sets us on the path to tragedy. But the representation of the event enables us to make it the turning point of our personal history, a kind of dark guiding star showing us the way. We are no longer protected when our bubble is shattered. The injury is real, of course, but its outcome is not independent of our will, since we have the power to make something out of it.

Dom was 18 when we was arrested by the Gestapo for being active in a student Christian youth group. Deported to Ravensbrück, he was subjected to the horrible torture that can be inflicted by a group of people organized into a hierarchical structure by relationships of violence. The young man learned to rummage in the garbage can near the SS prison, and this made it possible for him to survive until the Liberation. He was so weak after he returned to France that his mother had to hold him up when he went to see a doctor.

One day, as he passed a garbage can, Dom picked out some cherries that were still edible and ate them. The passersby were disgusted and berated him; he was called a pig and told he needed to have some dignity. The young man found it hard to understand how, in the course of a few weeks, behavior that had enabled him to survive Ravensbrück could have given rise to scorn in the streets of Paris. He slowly recovered from the huge trauma but would never dare to say that he was still drawn to garbage cans. The concept "garbage," imprinted in his memory, had come to mean hope for him. There was no way this could be explained to some obsessively finicky person for whom garbage simply means dirt. In both cases, the same object, garbage, takes on special importance. It stands out because of the preferential sensitivity of each observer. But for one of them it means "hope of life," whereas for the other it means "death by rotting." This is how people make things speak, reflecting their own histories.

When the trauma is flagrant and hyperconscious, we suffer from the blow but are as yet ignorant of the meaning that will be assigned to it in our personal history and in our surroundings.

Sometimes we even suffer without being aware of it. Emotional deprivation can constitute a lack without leading to a feeling of loss. A child may learn that he has lost his mother, that he will never see her again. To experience such a feeling he must have developed psychologically to the point where he has the concept of death, something that occurs gradually only from the age of 6 or 7 on. The concept of absolute death, a definitive void, gives rise to an anxiety that he will be able to combat by asking for help, idealizing the dead mother, or denying her death.

But when the child is too small to have such a concept, his sensory world is what is transformed. The familiar figure is no longer there but is vaguely replaced by someone unknown, a substitute attachment figure. This change in his world brings about a behavioral adaptation unbeknownst to him, just as we adapt to a lack of oxygen by breathing faster without being aware that we are doing so. We can speak in terms of trauma because what we are dealing with is a blow that shatters the child's world and damages him, but we can't speak of trauma to the extent that he can't yet represent the situation for himself in a way he can work with.[12] It is not a pain or even a loss. It is a slow disaffection, a malaise that changes the child all the more insidiously because he can't master, combat, or compensate for this emotional privation.[13]

In the long run, the child will adapt to this sensory impoverishment by a numbing of his perceptions. It becomes harder and harder to stimulate him, and, because his environment is no longer divided into a familiar setting and one that is unknown, his view of the world becomes blurry. He has more and more difficulty distinguishing between the people who stimulate him and those who make him anxious. This process of disaffection explains why an affiliation is necessary. When the sensory developmental supports in the child's environment are missing, the world no longer has an outline. And when there is no especially significant figure or event set in a historical context, when one piece of information is as good as another, the psychological world gets blurred and mental life loses structure. This is what happened to little Marilyn Monroe and did not happen to little Hans Christian Andersen.

Hence we can understand why children who empty themselves of life because of the emptiness around them often bring themselves back to life by inflicting pain on themselves. They bang their heads on the ground when people smile at them, bite themselves when they are spoken to. Later, as adults, they will provoke us by displaying their mutilations to us. Pain awakens them and forces them into reality, a reality that is cruel but arouses so much less anxiety than the emptiness of their world.

Logic leads us to wonder about the long-term effects of the early loss of one or both parents. This type of linear causality can be relevant for the study of the physics of materials, but psychological causalities are never-ending, like a waterfall, and are so numerous that we have to phrase the issue another way: the loss of a parent before a child is old enough to speak turns the child's sensory environment into a desert, and, when there are no parent figures or substitutes, the damage lasts a long time. On the other hand, if the small deprived child is provided with some supports for emotional and sensory resilience, he quickly resumes his development and may even make up for the delay. Which does not mean that, later, when he is able to speak, he will not think of himself as "someone who no longer has parents." And so the supports for affective resilience must be supplemented by cultural and verbal supports.

5. Connecting Mourning and Melancholy

It was not until 1917, in the middle of a world war, that Freud connected mourning with melancholy. The withdrawal of interest in the outer world and the loss of the ability to love and to work turn back into aggression against the person himself or herself and into self-depreciation and self-punishment.[14] The clinical picture of sadness had been determined before this, of course, but the cause was said to be humoral substances, black bile. From the end of the Middle Ages and the Renaissance, demonology explained this existential pain: "The devil takes advantage of human weaknesses, glad to get involved with the melancholy humor."[15]

Freud opened a new path by explaining that it was emotional loss of an actual person that created this feeling of a gray, empty world. A host of researchers then set out on this path, which quickly turned into a highway leading to the next point: "Every early bereavement, every emotional loss at an early age leads to lasting vulnerability and paves the way for depression in the adult years."[16]

Studies of resilience that take into account psychological difficulties throughout entire life cycles lead to different results. Some thirty children between the ages of 3 and 6 were followed after losing a parent in the preceding six months. Only two questions were to be answered. First, is there a mourning reaction after the death of a parent? Then, as the children were seen again at intervals until adulthood, the observers asked whether this group of children orphaned early on experienced more psychological problems than are normally found in the general population. Not only were the children questioned and tested, but the surviving parent, the family, and teachers were also examined.[17]

What is interesting is that this huge task led to huge disappointment. The problems appearing immediately after the bereavement were moderate: two children manifested anxiety, nightmares, hyperactivity, some self-accusation, one instance of self-harm, some scholastic delays, and withdrawal. If the method of observation had concerned only children regardless of context, the conclusions might have been that mourning

in a child under the age of 6 is very different from that of an adult—and
that is true. And the second conclusion would have been that the death
of a parent has almost no influence on a child's development—and that
is false. Since this method also took context into account, we can determine that the disturbed children were those whose surviving parent was
the most troubled, and that, in his state of deprivation, the child had
found no emotional support. It is therefore the suffering of the surviving parent that had caused the change in the child.

The prior relationship of the surviving parent and the child with the
dead parent also explains the difference in reactions. Children who had
achieved secure attachment[18] drew closer to the survivor when they saw
his or her grief. And even after adolescence, the death of a parent leads
to an improvement in the emotional relationship between the survivors: "Dad needs me. I didn't know he loved Mom so much. Grief has
brought us closer together."

The opposite conclusion is not rare either. The death of a parent drives
the survivors apart, especially in the case of a suicide, since guilt intrudes
on awareness.

In fact there are a great number of emotional scenarios, all of which lead
to different reactions. Children whose attachment was ambivalent often
attack the bereaved parent because his or her suffering is exacerbating the
child's own, whereas children with avoidant attachments protect themselves from suffering by becoming more distant than ever.

Finally, not many more problems are found in adults who were bereaved early in life than in the general population, which does not
mean that the children did not suffer or even that they resumed normal development.

When a 10-year-old child loses a parent, he has reached a level of
psychological development that enables him to conceptualize death as
a finality. Before this, deaths were games of make-believe in which
children fell down, acted as though they couldn't move, uttered funny
groans, or pretended to go on distant voyages. Between the ages of 6
and 9, the child is aware of the material reality of death.[19] He perceives
both death and also the emptiness brought about by the concept of a

definitive loss. His suffering is of a different kind, and different sup-ports, more sensory and social, are needed to help him pursue a course of development marked by the encroachment of death in his history.

Hence it is difficult to establish a linear causality and to say that people bereaved early on will be more prone to depression. Causes keep on occurring in a human life; a cause for happiness may follow a cause for unhappiness. The event that gives rise to suffering one day may be used to create happiness another day. The cascades of causes bring together opposing forces that may heal a child or make him worse, push him in a given direction or hold him back. But from this point on the supports are not only emotional. The more a child develops, the more those close to him distance themselves and the more—and more diverse—connections are formed. After his father and mother, the child discovers other close relationships in the family constellation: siblings, neighbors, pets, schoolmates. Later he will go in search of bonds out-side his family: in his social group and even further than that.

All of which makes it possible to say that, after an early bereavement, if the environment reorganizes itself around the child, he will be able to resume an altered development. But if there is no environment because the family has changed or disappeared, because the society has been destroyed or cultural beliefs get in the way of providing supports for resilience, then we have reason to be worried.

6. Is the Emptiness of Loss More Damaging
Than a Destructive Environment?

It is hard to differentiate between the harm done by absence and the toxicity of a destructive environment. In situations of parental failing, any evaluation is hard. When a couple keep on abusing their child, when an adult cheats a child out of his sexuality, when neglect shuts a child up alone in a closet, the developmental problems are so important that the child has to be removed for his protection.[20] This agonizing decision leads child-welfare workers to ask for reassuring recipes. I know of only two:

1. Separation protects the child but does not provide treatment for his trauma. A protection factor is not a resilience factor that invites the child to resume a kind of development.
2. When separation removes the child for his protection, this is an additional trauma. The child already traumatized by his parents retains the memory that those who wanted to protect him only attacked him all over again. So he puts the parental mistreatment in a perspective that enables him to preserve the image of parents who were kind in spite of everything, and he overemphasizes the memory of aggression on the part of those who protected him. This defense mechanism, dreadfully unjust as it is, is nevertheless habitual.

From the age of 8, Albert was locked out of his house whenever his parents went on vacation. They would close up the house, get into their big car, and leave the child alone outside without food, a bed, or keys because he would get the house dirty. It was several years before a neighbor came to understand this unlikely situation and alerted social services.

The child, who had suffered from cold, hunger, and filth when he was outdoors, suffered much more intensely from isolation in an institution in which no one spoke to him. When he was outside he had had a dog whose kennel he shared and whom he took care of. The social protection thus led to emotional isolation that exacerbated Albert's developmental problems to the point where, when he was 24, he considered suing the nice neighbor. She was shocked when she saw the formerly mistreated child tending his parents' garden in hopes of winning them over. It was not abuse that had made this young man abnormally kind but the cascade of traumas that lent the garden a relational significance he used to create the image of good parents: "They'll be happy when they get back, and they'll be nice to me."

There are no recipes, because linear reasoning makes hardly any sense. We can't say that separation protects the child, nor that he should be left in the abusive family because he wants to win them over. As many elements as possible in this boy's history and context have to be taken into account in order to discover which situation will encourage resilience and to avoid a more damaging one.

What seems logical is not always what protects the child and allows us to predict a resumption of development. The only reliable prediction in this area is when nothing is done. In that case we can anticipate changes "leading to major psychological difficulties, intellectual deficiency, violence, and behavioral and psychiatric problems."[21] It is not his parents' poverty that changes the child but emotional isolation, the absence of routines. A child left alone grows weak, because all learning becomes a source of anxiety. Insecure as he is, he does not take pleasure in discovery. Unable to feel the pleasure of depending on an adult he loves to snuggle up against, he can only orient himself to his own body, swaying back and forth, sucking his thumb, uttering sounds all alone, and thus depriving himself of developmental supports.

Even the very act of thinking becomes a source of anxiety since, in order to understand, a new concept has to be created. And so all change makes the child anxious. In the absence of emotional routines he keeps himself from thinking so as not to suffer too much. And when parental failings come early on and last a long time, when, unfortunately, this unsupportive environment continues, the child fixes in memory a kind of self-centered development, incorporating an emptiness, an emotional desert, into his mind. The only pieces of information he can bear will come from his own body.

In such situations, children's growth is severely handicapped: 77 percent will suffer from serious intellectual deficiency; only 32 percent will get a vocational training qualification[22]; and 95 percent, not having had a childhood, will be afraid of becoming parents. Panicked at the thought of having a child, they will do anything to avoid this and will suffer for it. When they do become parents, they are so anxious that they make the child anxious in turn. Such a catastrophe is predictable when nothing is done; when cultural stereotypes stigmatize these children; when they are said to be monstrous, screwed up, permanently retarded, prone to delinquency; when the government does not build the kinds of institutions that would enliven them; when exhausted or malformed families prevent the weaving of any affective ties; or when adults in a position of responsibility, believing that these children cannot possibly be redeemed, provide them with no supports for resilience.

7. Blowing on an Ember of Resilience May Give It New Life

I have had occasion to see some seriously impaired children come back to life. I'm thinking of a brilliant grandmother, very poor but rich in affection, who was willing to take in three filthy kids from a Timisoara orphanage because she thought living alone was really too hard for her. A year later the three boys were totally changed. Feeling responsible for the grandmother, they had repaired her house, planted a garden, and built a pigpen. They did the laundry and the dishes, rallying round the old lady who said, with a toothless smile, that she missed the time when she was able to work. By restoring the vulnerable old woman's property, they restored their own self-esteem. The well-kept house and the happy grandmother became the proof of their competence and their generosity.

A small group of abandoned orphans has been followed in an orphanage in Vidra, Rumania.[23] As soon as they were able to bask in an emotional milieu structured by routinized interactions, most of them resumed development. Their motor skills improved, they caught up verbally, and even their relational difficulties faded away. The children gradually learned to maintain eye contact, to respond with smiles, and to seek out the affection they needed. Not all of them recovered in the same way; individual differences were pronounced. Some of them caught up in language use within a few months, while others "preferred" to begin by growing bigger and taller. Some smiled a lot, while others went through a stage of hyperactivity and still others made no gains.[24]

These many examples demonstrate that it is our scientific culture that fragments knowledge in order to control it better. A real child can't be divided into pieces; he is a total being whose physical improvement is connected to progress in language and whose intelligence is connected to his emotional life.

We may "challenge the widespread idea that early experience has a disproportionate effect on later development."[25] The child learns his environment, incorporating it into his memory of the first months and in the ways he develops. When the sensory bubble provided by the family is well structured by emotional and behavioral routines, the child grows alongside these sensory structures. When such routines are not established during the early months, the child cannot organize himself. When a child has been disorganized by the disorganization of his surroundings, structures must be intentionally placed around him if we are to see a resumption of development. Each child has his own way of responding, but when deprivation has gone on too long, when there has been total psychological extinction or the new environment has not blown on the embers of resilience, the little one will find it hard to come back to life.

8. How to Get an Abused Child to Repeat the Abuse

A clinical observation like this makes it impossible to uphold the stereotypical view that when a child was mistreated at an early age, he has learned that violence is a normal way to solve problems and will therefore repeat the abuse. We must acknowledge that abused children often alternate between icy vigilance and explosions of violence against those close to them. Always on the alert, they are serious, attentive to the slightest behavioral sign on the part of the adult, and tend to go to extremes.[26] A wrinkling of the eyebrows, a tension in the voice, a barely noticeable pinching of the mouth will be signs of danger for them. Impulses suddenly go off in all directions, against someone else or against the child himself, since he hasn't learned to give form to his emotions.

This kind of relational learning, of incorporation of an emotional style, takes place from the earliest months and explains why, in a group of abused children, almost all will have developed an insecure, distant, ambivalent, or confused attachment between 12 and 18 months.

These children who have adapted to a setting in which every piece of information is a threat say little as they grow up and don't invest themselves in school. This emotional style, imprinted in their memory by the behavioral habits of an environment in which confused attachment is combined with violence, is an adaptation, not a resilience factor, since such children learn to see only the threats in the world and to respond to them.[27]

When violence is repeated in closed families, the child's behavioral responses become fixed and characterize his style—as long as the system isn't opened up.

I still have the frightening memory of children with shaved heads, motionless and mute, behind the bars of the luxurious institution where they were confined. After having been abused by their parents, they were abused by society, which separated them for their protection and then shut them away in a chateau with a big park where no one came to see them. Used to receiving only threats, they replied to simple commands by trying to attack the adults. The relationship was completely perverted, since the adults, feeling threatened in turn by the children, likewise alternated between icy vigilance and explosions of rage.

Certain studies observe that 100 percent of abused children become violent, whereas others find that "only" 70 percent do.[28] In every group, 65 percent of the children will attain a trusting attachment, a way of loving in which, since they feel lovable, they dare to charm the unknown. In some groups of abused children, none of them, zero percent, have attained this level. The difference is astonishing. All these scientific studies therefore allow us to evaluate the following notion: abusing a child does not make him happy! After this shattering discovery, we may wonder whether such quantitative variation in results is due to variation in environment.

Two reference points show the extent to which learned violence depends on the environment more than on the child. If the environment is changed, the child changes in terms of attainments. Assaulted and neglected children[29] are not only impaired by a greater number of more or less serious cerebral lesions, but they also have more accidents than the general population. We can't draw the conclusion that they have acquired the violence molecule predisposing them to accidents, but when we link clinical observation with scientific studies we understand that these unfortunate children, whose inner world has been invaded by images of suffering, are somehow cut off from reality and unable to analyze it correctly. And so, when a difficult situation arises, they treat it confusedly or give up on themselves in a way that amounts to suicide.

9. Estelle's Sad Happiness Was Still a Form of Progress

IQ measures not the intelligence of the child but the rapidity of his development in a given milieu.[30] This test provides a reference point of intellectual adaptation in a culture where school plays an important role. Some researchers have sanctified the IQ test, making it an intellectual hierarchy, which explains why others have fought to disqualify it in a battle of ideas that is more ideological than scientific.

Rigid thinking sets the data in stone. But when we observe these children over time, we see that those who give themselves over to accidents no longer do so once they feel loved. As for the measurement that shows intellectual liveliness like a flash camera, true today but false tomorrow, it reveals that the child's awakening mounts like an arrow as soon as the environment assigns a relational value to knowledge. We play at speech in order to exchange emotions, we learn to read with someone we love, we gain knowledge in order to share abstract worlds. The IQ number is interpersonal: it is an emotional encounter that varies greatly according to the environment in which the child is steeped.[31]

This is why the IQ continues to be an indicator of resilience as long as it is not highjacked ideologically, as though intelligence were a feature of the brain or the characteristic of a social group. The intelligence of the resilient child is above all relational. If there is no humanity around him, for whom is he supposed to make the effort to understand? He will seek to solve only immediate problems. On the other hand, as soon as someone is willing to love him, the wounded child is so eager to establish an emotional relationship with that person that he will submit to his or her beliefs solely in order to have some ideas they can share. I know abandoned children who have espoused adults' ideologies just to please them and exist in their minds. These children took up careers they didn't like simply so as to be able to discuss their jobs from time to time with the welfare worker who was willing to love them.

Estelle's father never spoke. He remained enclosed in the pain of having been expelled from Algeria. It was very striking to see this huge,

somber, harsh man explode over trivialities. The entire family lived in
a small house in the middle of the forest, where the very trees were part
of the confinement. The mother, intimidated, kept silent. "My mother
is gray," Estelle used to say. In this woodland tomb, the only moments
of gaiety were provided by the two older brothers. This is why, when
they climbed into her bed one night, Estelle didn't understand right
away. As she grew up, she then experienced several years of emotional
and sexual confinement in what it is difficult to call a family.

By the time the father died, the two brothers had found honest
work. Estelle found staying alone with her mother unbearable, but she
was also unable to bear the thought of going out into the world, which
frightened her a lot. She spent several sad years in a suburban hostel,
attempting suicide several times so as to kill that life, until the day she
met an older man with whom she dared to live.

Estelle felt better being together with this man she didn't love, because
he gave her a sense of security. She needed someone to take on the maternal role no one had ever played for her. As a result their sex life was mediocre, but Estelle forgave her pathetic lover because of her great need
for his attachment to her. He was an accountant and paid for her training
in accountancy, though what she dreamed of was literature. He provided
a great deal of support. Today she has a career she doesn't like, in the
company of a man she doesn't love: she is doing much better!

Allowing resilience to develop means providing developmental support for an injured person. Without this man Estelle would have known
only terror, sensory confinement, the incest of her two brothers, and
fear of other people. Thanks to the accountant, she has resumed a kind
of development that strengthens and reassures her.

And so we can't say that a trauma gives rise to a characteristic form
of damage, such as incest supposedly leading to prostitution or abuse
leading to abuse. These tendencies appear only when nothing is done
to help the injured person. Estelle's story enables us to think differently:
a trauma may undergo progressive changes, with different outcomes
depending on the possibilities made available to the injured person for
forming different bonds.

10. Resilience of Swiss Street Children in the Sixteenth Century

Now that biographies are beginning to be studied scientifically, we find that in all periods a great many people have had to deal with such ruptures. Traumatic wounds were common in former centuries, and the accounts of these injuries reveal how some people managed to emerge from hell and lead a human life in spite of everything.

Thomas Platter was a wandering scholar in the sixteenth century.[32] Born near Zermatt, he nearly died because his mother was unable to nurse him. He was given cow's milk, which he suckled for five years through a horn in which a hole had been made. His father died when Thomas was still an infant. His mother, ruined, gave him over to a sister who lived on a farm and made him a farmhand from the time he was 7 years old. The child, who was very weak, was knocked about by the goats, beaten by the watchmen, injured in frequent accidents, and scalded on one occasion. His feet froze because he had no wooden shoes for walking in the snow, but his greatest suffering was thirst.

When street children are questioned,[33] they describe the extent to which thirst is a constant concern, often even a torture. But a few years later, when they are asked to tell about their difficult moments, they choose from among their memories, relating only plausible events and forgetting how thirsty they were.

We should not be surprised by this reconstructive aspect of memory, which also explains its therapeutic potential. By choosing logical memories and forgetting meaningless events, they give coherence to their image of the past and feel more of a sense of identity. The thirst that tormented them for such a long period has no place in their recollections. School, however, becomes a major event in their accounts because it constituted their first steps toward socialization.

In Thomas Platter's day teachers beat children dreadfully. They picked them up from the ground by their ears and were especially fond of hitting them on their fingertips, where the feeling of pain is most acute. Platter went to school in the daytime and begged at night. "I was often very hungry and very cold prowling around until midnight, singing in the darkness to get bread."[34] People often gave him stale bread, and he scraped off the mold. He ate with pleasure, yet the delight was not physical. It was not the bread he enjoyed; the fact that he was brave enough to swallow a moldy piece of food kindled hope for a bit of life in him. The meaning of a fact depends on its context: eating moldy bread when he was alone in the street provided a little hope, whereas if Platter had had to eat the same moldy bread living with a rich family, he would have been mortified.

After attending school for several months he was still living in the street, where he discovered the protective value of the group. These "troupes" of eight or nine children between the ages of 10 and 15 covered extraordinary distances on foot. Thomas set out from Zurich, came to Dresden, stayed for awhile in Munich, and returned to Dresden. He grew up and saw something of the world, learning the dialects of the regions he passed through to the point where people no longer understood him when he returned. These children are attacked physically, exploited, scorned, and regularly insulted. The older they grow, the more ashamed they are of having to beg.

Near Lake Constance Thomas was astounded to see "on the bridge some little Swiss peasants with their while smocks: ah! how happy I was; I thought I was in heaven."[35] He went to school here and there. At age 18 he couldn't read but told himself that he would study or die. And so he learned Latin, Greek, and Hebrew with the fervor of the self-taught: everything, too much, all in disorder. He became a rope maker, married, lost his wife, remarried, took care of numerous children, and pursued his studies. He eventually became a "learned master," director of a prestigious school in Basel, and rector of the cathedral. One of his children, Félix Platter, was a physician at the court of Henri IV, a friend of Montaigne's, and a famous writer.

This is a common life story in Europe at this time. Platter did not transmit abuse to his children. Is it possible that what he transmitted to them was the rage to learn and the fever of happiness? This kind of reconstruction, of course, goes hand in hand with anxiety and exhaustion, but no one ever said that resilience was an easy path.

What astonishes me is little Thomas's amazement at seeing the white smocks of well-bred children. Like any lightning rod, he received the lightning only because he was its privileged receptor. Sensitive to this kind of image, he perceived the children better than others did; he was even hoping for them. He felt he was in heaven when he saw the white smocks, whereas another abandoned child might have felt hatred or envy. What made Thomas aspire to white smocks and school, this boy who begged, slept outdoors, and was illiterate?

The reason is probably that an entire part of his personality had been shaped by events that, imprinted in his memory, had made him sensitive to this type of life project. His ideal self, his aspirations, and probably his daydreams revealed what could still make him happy although he had known only an incredible series of misfortunes.

In our modern world, street children, whose numbers are increasing considerably,[36] have an adventure like that of Thomas Platter in the sixteenth century. Before going on the street, did they experience early interactions that led to a difficult initial attachment? And, once on the street, were they assaulted even more than Thomas was?

Everyone working with street children has noted their physical illnesses, their frequent "accidental" injuries, and the difficulty in approaching them and making a connection with them. And yet what impresses us are the children who, despite the blows of fate and the horror of daily life, manage to hold on and even to escape. These are the children who need to be studied if we are to understand what happened inside them and in their environment, so that we can better help those who find it hard to construct themselves.

11. They Felt Lovable Because They Had Been Loved and Had Learned to Hope

The twentieth century was covered with the shame of lethal ideologies. These tragic operettas, each more charming than the next, led to death. German children, adorable little blondes 8 to 12 years old, were beautiful when playing war in short pants and sailors' caps. Almost all of them were dead several years later, and those who survived became torturers so as to impose the operetta in which they believed. Soviet children were so pretty with their little golden-haired Ukrainian heads, their slanting Asiatic eyes, and their tanned Georgian skin. While they were waving their handkerchiefs to make a declaration of love to the little father of nations, the invisible police were deporting tens of millions of people who would die in secret, maintaining their allegiance to the vaudeville that was killing them.

We can confidently predict that the twenty-first century will be the century of population movements. A few increasingly rich countries several hours' journey away from increasingly poorer countries, forgotten cultural traditions, groups made up of random agglomerations, shattered family structures, and the abandonment of over one hundred million children on the planet will most certainly trigger survival reactions and flight into more structured countries.[37]

Whether they are the Swiss children of Platter's time, the little Europeans set out on the streets after the war, or the children of Southeast Asia today, all those who escaped carried out a common program of resilience. Unbelievably dirty, injured, sick, drugged, and sometimes prostituted, they all worked to repair their self-esteem. Those who didn't manage that learned violence and despair, but those who were able to undertake the task of resilience had learned hope before being abandoned.

In the course of their early interactions a trace was set down in their memory, the feeling of having already been helped in their ordeal when they were very small. They had no real recollections, no images of an attachment figure taking care of them, no remembrance of words promising assistance, and yet they felt lovable. Because they had been loved, they had a hope of being helped. Secure attachment is most easily imprinted in the earliest months; attaining this feeling, this relational style, makes things easier but is not a matter of destiny. What is not set in place when it is most easy to come by can be worked on later, though more slowly.

Hope, once learned and imprinted in memory, creates the ability to dream of the future: "I'm unhappy today, my reality is desolate, but because someone already loved me, I'm going to be loved. What do I have to do to meet the person who will be willing to help me?" Dreams usually bring back the traces of the past, but when hope has been learned, dreams of anticipation are the imaginary constructions of our wishes. We can dream to protect ourselves or to imagine ourselves. Taking refuge in daydreams is not always an active matter. It is a balm when reality is painful, whereas active daydreaming is a sample of the way to make ourselves happy, a creative activity pinning down hope in a desperate world. Happiness, of course, is played out virtually in a scenario of images, but this imagined scene gives form to hope. Without this kind of imaginary activity, wounded children would remain stuck in the present, bogged down in the perception of things. This is what happens when children become agitated because they are not allowed to dream or when consumers are subjected to instant gratification.

This is why the resilient children of the street dream of their future in a context in which they should logically fall into despair. Those who adapt too well to a terrifying reality are content to respond to the present. They become thieves in order to survive, use drugs to calm themselves, and set up in business as prostitutes. But those who have learned hope project onto the screen of their inner theater an ideal dream in which they assign themselves the role of the loved child, the renowned hero, or the adult who is simply happy.

This imaginary work saves them from horror, freeing them from their context and inviting them to get busy by offering an ideal self to be realized. What is remarkable is that this launching of resilience, its emergence, springs forth in the imagination. Taking care of these children, feeding them, and washing them is a physical necessity, of course, but it does not trigger a process of resilience. Just as a traumatic event requires a blow in the real world followed by a representation of that blow, we can say that resilience calls for a repairing of the real blow followed by a repairing of the representation of that blow. A child who has been washed and fed and bandaged will do better in the here and now, and clearly one has to do those things. But if the bandaging is not felt, imbued with meaning and direction, the child will return to the street. Everything will have to be done over again from the beginning, only this time the child is blamed "after all we've done for him."

12. Giving Children the Right to Give

When we wander aimlessly and without daydreaming, we are prey to the here and now. But if the child is given the opportunity to form a representation of what has happened, we can set in motion a process of resilience.

We must first free the child from immediate need so as to help him experience the representation we are going to work out with him. It's surprising to see an adult organizing a philosophy club with street children. A naive observer might even become indignant: "They're sick, alone in the world, with no school and no protection, and you're talking to them about Plato or Confucian detachment!" When we speak of these abstract thinkers with the children, we're inviting them to transcendence, suggesting that they can conquer a world other than the one they have to deal with. If the intellectual exchange takes place within a bond of friendship, we can witness a transformation.

Rafaël was perfectly adapted to the street. He knew how to steal a handbag without getting caught, how to wash cars stopped at red lights, how to beg, get a bit high, sell cigarettes, and sometimes sell himself. He survived without suffering too much and didn't realize that he was heading toward desocialization.

Although he was over six feet tall, Cornelio didn't frighten the children. He would sit down on a little stone wall and begin a philosophical discussion with them. An ordinary comment would have scared them, accustomed as they were to hearing scathing, moralizing remarks.

A talk on the topic "Are you free in the street?" had aroused bursts of laughter, anger, and a lot of astonishment. Little Rafaël came away from it thunderstruck: so it was possible to live some other way! Some time after that, the police caught him, and this time Rafaël didn't react the way he usually did. Instead of playing tough, he went over to the cop and said, "Slap me, please."

Bewildered, the policeman felt his aggression melting away, and he felt like chatting with Rafaël instead of questioning him harshly. They shared their views on the family, the meanness of adults, and how much fun school was. The child didn't at all want to be slapped. But he knew that, by asking for this, he would disarm the policeman. Empathy, the ability to put ourselves in someone else's place, is surely an essential component of resilience. Putting ourselves in someone else's place enables us to calm him down, or possibly to help him or to delight him by putting on a show for him. Wait! Why do we say "putting on a show for him"? Are we giving something to someone when we go onstage? Could this be a way of re-establishing equality when we've been dominated? By sharing our inner world, would we become normal?

In any case, at some point a trauma will turn into a recollection.[38] So is it possible not to do anything with it? If we make it recur again and again, if we brood over it, we can only amplify it and become a prisoner of the past. But if we make it into a show, a reflection, a relationship, even a burst of laughter, we become someone who gives and thereby repairs his injured self-esteem. I would have to check this, but I believe that, among the necessary rights of children, we have forgotten to give kids the right to give. Fortunately, resilient children take this right and, in so doing, transform the memory of their trauma into a relational tool.

Why do 4-year-olds enjoy giving adults the drawings they have just made? Partly because they thereby establish an emotional relationship, and partly because it is with an object that comes from very deep inside them that they become loved and make those they love happy. In giving, the child feels big, good, strong, and generous. His self-esteem, enhanced by the gift, leads to a feeling of well-being and forms a link in the connection.

Almost all street children have discovered this right to give. It would be more accurate to say that the children who, later on, have become resilient were the ones who, at the moment of greatest despair, gave themselves the right to give. With the money earned by begging or watching cars, or in little business transactions, they bought food or medicine for the weakest among them.[39] Many street children bring a little money to their isolated mother, and some even pay their own school fees! Being a grownup when you are 8 years old and struggling to survive gives you an amazing feeling of quiet strength, even if this is a rather odd way for a child to develop.

13. We Can Speak of Trauma Only When There Has Been a Psychological Near-Death Experience

In the West, the life of one child out of four will be rent by trauma before the age of 10. By the end of his or her life, one adult out of two will have experienced such a rupture and will end up broken by the trauma or will have transformed it.[40] We may conjecture that, in regions where socialization is less stable, the number of those injured is even higher.

In the nineteenth century, the ferment of social reorganization resulting from industrialization must have led to many traumas. The countryside, being more stable, offered its inhabitants more underpinnings. Immigration from the interior uprooted the people of Brittany, the Morvan, and Picardy, who, in order to survive, agreed to undertake the industrial adventure at an exorbitant human cost.

I have known men who arrived at Montparnasse Station with enough money to last two days. They didn't speak French and were unfamiliar with our practices. Some boys would wriggle through mineshafts as early as the age of 12, and little sweepers from Savoy would be let down on ropes into chimneys; domesticated little girls were sometimes well received and other times sorely tormented.

This immense ordeal was not a trauma insofar as these men and children retained their dignity and felt accepted as long as they hardened themselves to bad conditions and learned the language and customs of the "country" that took them in. They were shored up by charitable groups that invented rituals: the Saturday-night dance and the Sunday soccer match. Popular stories and songs about their troubles related the edifying history of a child from a good background sleeping in the street and exploited by thieves but nevertheless becoming happy in the end as part of a social group. The suffering was great, but there was no rupture. These men and women kept their own personalities under very harsh circumstances.

Since we know, today, that our identity is structured by personal and cultural narratives, it would be interesting to ask which events, set down in memory, enable us to shape a life story. After a great ordeal emotions normally undergo change. We feel relieved, even proud, when we have overcome the obstacle, but confusion follows a traumatic event: our ability to think clearly is slowed down so that we can't make sense of the world, and our mental fogginess leads us to focus on a single detail that points to impending death, holding us spellbound to the point where everything else is obscured. In this psychic near-death experience[41] all we have left is a few sparks of life that we must transform into the embers of resilience.

14. Storytelling Enables Us to Sew Up the Pieces of a Torn Self

Undertaking the task of resilience means once again shedding light on the world and giving it back its coherence. The tool that makes this possible is called *narration*.

A story, of course, can't be told if it has no basis. We have to have been aware of the explosions of traumatic reality and set them down as memories, connected and reorganized into logical time sequences. This mental effort must be addressed to someone with whom we are emotionally involved. That is to say, in even the smallest account each person is a co-author of the story.

Children love the way stories begin: "Once upon a time" is a happy event, a promise of happiness, an emotional engagement in which the speaker announces verbal adventures to be shared with the listener. We begin to enjoy ourselves as soon as we see the cake, way before we taste it. The announcement of pleasure is a pleasure in itself.

But wounded children can't say "Once upon a time." For them, sharing a misfortune means dragging loved ones into your own sorrow, and how is that supposed to bring comfort? To share a misfortune is to suffer all over again, unless . . . unless taking part in the relating of a disaster is precisely not the same as sharing it. The choice of words, the arrangement of memories, and the quest for aesthetic effect entail the mastery of emotions and the reworking of our image of what has happened to us.

"Did you see the movie *Life Is Beautiful*?" asks Rémy Puyelo. "The hero is with his son in a concentration camp. A soldier asks, 'Does anyone understand German?' The hero of the film, who doesn't understand a word of German, offers his services as a translator. But the version he gives his son is turned into a game: he uses splitting to set up a countertraumatic storyline."[42] The child would have been numbed by the soldier's incomprehensible or terrifying account. If his father had translated the reality, he would have communicated the trauma, but by playing with the translation he was able to avoid doing so.

"Splitting" is a good way to describe this narrative process that, in the face of a threat, divides the account into two incompatible parts. One part is confused, like the part of the mind that is in its death throes, while the other, still alive, becomes a source of light and even merriment. When the account of the trauma takes this form it can bring healing, since it enables us to remain in the human world, providing a verbal bridge to other people and strengthening this thin emotional thread. When a wounded person speaks this way he affirms himself and takes up his position. As soon as he undertakes the task of a shared story, he breaks the spell of the filthy beast that had enchanted him and drawn him toward death. He blows on the ember of resilience, the part of himself that is still alive.

Thus we can categorize different types of traumatic storytelling. People who are spellbound by what threatens them remain its prisoner, spending their time repeating the same story and describing the same image. Those, however, who articulate a split narrative bear witness to the setting in motion of a process of resilience:

> If I tell about the scabbed-over part of myself, I'll drag the people I love into death. They'll reject me, or, what is worse, they'll go down with me. So to save myself and them I'll tell only the bearable part that's still alive in me. Little by little a bridge will form between me and others. By putting into words what happened to me, I'll slowly shed light on the confused part of my personality, and this verbal strengthening will "narcissize" me.[43] I'll gradually become whole again.

We are all co-authors of the personal accounts of those who have been wounded in their souls. When we silence them, we leave them in the death throes of the scarred part of their self, but when we listen to them as though we were receiving a revelation, we run the risk of transforming their story into a myth. After all, these survivors are ghosts. They have been close to death, have come to know it, brushed up against it, and escaped it. They strike us as being initiates into a mystery and make us anxious the way ghosts do. Moreover, they themselves say they have come back from hell. If we worship them and offer blanket approval, we get in the way of the psychological work they are doing as they speak, since their story then becomes emblematic, veneered, and anecdotal, impeding thought in the manner of stereotypes that turn truth into stone.

This is what we see today with the weakening of the terms *genocide* or *crime against humanity*. The expression "it's violent in the extreme" and the slogan equating the French riot squad with the Nazi SS trivialize trauma and silence the injured person when they refer to a mere jolt. Passive acceptance of a traumatic account hinders intersubjective work. The walking wounded of life understand that the other person thinks of their trauma as an ordinary disruption. In the face of the vastness of the task they must undertake, they give up and prefer to say nothing.

The listener, too, is uneasy, since he can neither express his disgust for the wound nor deflect his relish for the horror into hysteria. He yawns when the sufferer describes his pain, putting the atrocity of the crime into a more tolerable perspective.

There is only one way to care for a traumatized person and calm the people around him: understanding. Immediately after an accident, just being present and speaking to the victim can be enough to make him feel safe. It is only later that the coherence of the narrative will bring coherence to the event. Children who have managed to become resilient adults have been assisted in making sense of their injuries. The work of resilience consisted in recalling the shocks in such a way that they become images, actions, and words in order to interpret the rupture.

15. The Imprint of Reality and the Search for Memories

Contrary to what people think, very small children have exact recollections of their experiences. But since not everything can be remembered, they create images only of what has made an impression on
them. For a little 3-year-old Parisian, the war in Afghanistan or the
world-championship victory of a handball team do not set down memories, whereas the routine consisting of saying a prayer at bedtime or visit-
ing his grandmother every Sunday stabilizes his mental world and leads
him to expect the next prayer or visit. As a result, on the day when his
parents are so upset by the victory of the handball team that they forget
the bedtime prayer, this break in routine takes on the feeling of an event,
and the associated emotion registers that evening in the child's memory.

The memory of a 3-year-old is as well organized as that of an older
child of 10 or 12, but the routines and events that make an impression
on him aren't the same. A child of 8 can describe in detail the memory
of his first plane trip when he was 3 as long as his parents made it into a
stimulating emotion. Even a child of 2 can recognize the game that made
him burst out laughing when he played it a year earlier. Adults forget
how reliable their childhood memory is. It becomes schematized over
time, of course, and loses emotional resonance as it is revised: we recall
the image of the event as a mimed story, slowly forgetting the feelings
that accompanied it, though it was these that created the sense of special importance.

Children who were traumatized—abused or abandoned—before
they could talk all develop a problem with expressing emotions: they
jump at the slightest noise, are distressed by the slightest separation,
are frightened by the least new thing, and try to freeze up in order to
suffer less. Changes in the brain, inscribed by trauma, hinder emotional
control and make the child easy to confuse. At this stage of development
every emotion-laden event brings on a sensory chaos, and this is why
the child selectively perceives whatever arouses aggression in him, for
example, speaking in a loud voice or a bit too much self-assertion. The
child adapts to the view of the world imprinted on his biological memory,
and this is what he responds to. He reacts aggressively because he has

been made fearful, or else he escapes into a kind of hyperactive head-long flight.

The strategy of resilience, in contrast, would involve learning to express feelings in a different way. Coordinated action and the behavioral expression, visual or verbal, of the child's inner world lead to his once again gaining control over his emotions.

Posttraumatic psychic life is thus filled with the snippets of memory with which we have to reconstruct our past, but also with an acquired hypersensitivity to a kind of world that will characterize our life from now on. With what bricks taken from reality will we construct our imagination? With what events will we constitute our memories? With what words will we try to regain a place in the world of human beings?

A child assaulted in the preverbal period, therefore, can't perform the same psychological task as a child traumatized at a time when he can rework the experience in words. When the rupture occurred before the advent of speech, the environment is what has to be repaired in order to sew the child back together again. But with a child injured after having learned to talk, the work must be done with the way he conceptualizes what happened.

Each recollection makes us into someone new, because every event chosen to be a brick of memory alters the way we think of ourselves. This process of construction is filled with hope, since memories evolve with time and with storytelling. But the inner world of trauma also depends on the inner world of the person who is confided in and on the emotional charge that the culture assigns to the traumatizing event. This means that the way everyone—absolutely everyone—speaks of the trauma is part of the traumatization, whether bandaging it or ulcerating it. One woman told me how mortified she was when she heard the person sitting next to her on a bus saying with a laugh, "It's impossible to rape a woman, because you can run faster in a hiked-up skirt than with pants around your ankles." Did this joke mean that people would smile if she told the story of her rape? All she could do was keep silent.

Every word claims to illuminate a piece of reality. But in so doing it transforms the event, attempting to clarify something that would otherwise remain in the realm of confusion or of perception without an associated concept. To speak of the past is to interpret it, to ascribe a meaning to a shattered world, to a disorder that is hard to understand and to which one can no longer respond. We need to speak so as to restore order, but in speaking we interpret the event in any one of a thousand directions.

Alongside memories of images that are incredibly precise yet surrounded by fog there is another source of memory: the scenarios of recollections created by speech. The visual memories of our children appear even before they are able to speak. They are more exact than those of adults, but they express a child's point of view. Each person, observing the world from his or her own position, sees different images, and all of these are true. These schemas remain etched in the child's memory, but when the story is shared with an adult the emotion associated with the representation depends on the way it is discussed with that adult.[44]

Let's play "pirates" with two groups of 5-year-old children. The experiment involves giving one group only cut-and-dried explanations: "We're going to go behind the chair," "We're going to raise the hand that's holding the sword," "We're going to open this box." With the other group, however, the commentary is emotion-laden: "I'm taking my heavy sword," "I'm attacking the wicked pirates," "What's this I see? A mysterious pirate chest," "Oh, what beautiful gems! What marvelous colors: the gold, the red of the rubies, the green of the emeralds."

Several months later we meet with the two groups again and ask them to replay the scenario that was made up the previous time. Only the group steeped in speech charged with feeling is able to call up many memories, while the others, who merely got a simple explanation of the game, can come up with only a few behavioral patterns.[45]

In both cases the memories are there, but they live on in different ways. The recollections of this game will be a component of each child's identity, but they will vary according to the way the environment presented them. This storing up of memories probably explains why traumas form lucid memories for some people but remain befogged for others.

16. When an Image Memory Is Exact, the Way It Is Spoken of Depends on the Environment

If the recollection of the trauma is clear, this is because the event made an impression and the environment articulated it clearly. When a shock leads to the incursion Freud spoke of, the inner world is shattered to the point where one's familiar landmarks are lost.

The repatriation of 500,000 American soldiers from Vietnam went very badly. Not only had the war been an immense ordeal, but in addition the battles had no meaning for most of these young men who wondered what they were doing there. After the Viet Cong took Saigon the retreat was chaotic, full of shouting, insults, and injustices. But what mattered most is that the retreat was an additional ordeal for these exhausted men who had been through so much mindless horror. They felt rejected by the country they thought they were defending. The veterans did not get a hero's welcome. On the contrary, they had to endure accusations that made them out as shameful criminals. Everything conspired to make the images engraved in their memory into a trauma. "According to official statistics, the number of violent deaths (suicides and homicides) among American veterans was higher than during the conflict."[46]

When trauma is ongoing, the event is less distinctive because it is numbed by its very ordinariness. And when the victim, in order to feel better, needs to repair the image of the aggressor to whom he is connected, his memory takes on a different emotional connotation. Many abused children retain an especially sharp memory of certain scenes of violence, but others, to the utter amazement of witnesses, claim they were never mistreated.

Not a day went by that Sylvain was not beaten. His foster mother spent a lot of money on whips, belts, and brooms to be broken over the child's head. When she punched him her hand hurt too much, so of course she had to buy these instruments. The little orphan felt he was one too many in this family. He was made to feel that he cost too much to feed, that his cot was taking up too much room in the closet where he slept among the clothes hanging there, and that he had done a poor job of keeping things tidy, cooking, filling out official papers, and taking care of the family's two daughters. So, clearly, the foster mother had to take a whip to this 10-year-old child to "make him understand."

When the little girls were older, the parents took them on a vacation, leaving Sylvain outside on the doorstep. Neighbors intervened, and, at the age of 14, Sylvain was placed in an institution where he was very happy. He caught up scholastically, learned the trade of cabinetry, and married a neighbor with whom he had two children.

His wife is astounded when he states that it was very nice of his foster family to keep him for such a long time. Yet the beatings had been inflicted daily and systematically: a slap or a blow with the broom for a plate not properly put away, a noodle dish badly cooked, the bathtub not scrubbed clean. The thrashing would come without a word: no threat, justification, or accompanying remark. Sylvain's kindness, his impulse to reach out to others, had made him a resilient young man whose protective defenses enabled him to resist making a mental contract with past trauma: "I have no accounts to settle," he told his amazed wife when she saw how attentive he was to his former foster mother.

The imprint of the real on the brain, the memory trace, is continually being reworked by the self-observation that constitutes memory. Beginning at 18 months, the development of the nervous system makes it possible to establish a preverbal memory, an image representation.

A little girl aged 2 years and 3 months suddenly changed her behavior. A lively, smiling child, she had become stiff, serious, almost inert. A child of this age can't tell her story or draw a picture of it; only the abrupt behavioral change revealed her disturbing transformation. At the age of 6 she drew an explicit picture, on which she wrote: "Grandfather." Slowly encouraged to speak out, she related what had happened.[47] The grandfather's confession, four years later, explained the dramatic behavioral change and confirmed that a memory of a precise image can be established before the mastery of speech.

But this traumatic memory is distinctive: it puts the spotlight on the aggressor in fine detail but leaves a shadow around him. Although nowadays we know that children's autobiographical memory is much more reliable than was previously thought, it must be added that the way child victims express their image memories is highly dependent on the way adults get them to speak.

Myrna was 4 when she was in Beirut during the Lebanese war. Games that had nothing to do with violence had made her a trusting child who said, one day, "I saw the end of the gun. I saw the stone broken by the noise. It made me bleed a lot. The man with the beard is the one who made the noise." Her childlike vocabulary didn't prevent her from clearly describing the image memories, as long as the adult allowed them to come forth.

Many adults live in such a grown-up world that they have forgotten how children talk. And so they direct the conversation by asking grown-up questions in which the reference points of memory are essentially social: "Was it on Djallil Street or Aboukir Street?" The child is surprised, because these reference points are meaningless for her. She might reply, "Djallil," from which the adult concludes that the child will say anything because there never was a Djallil Street. In fact it is the adult who has elicited the wrong answer by drawing the child into a world of references that are clear for grown-ups but vague for a child.

We have just seen how the pirate game led to the suggestion that an entire section of memory is determined by verbalization. Not only do adults' words fix images in children's memories, but all the biases of the culture do so as well. Our stereotypes, repeated over and over, structure the child's verbal environment and take part in the construction of the most sincerely held memories. In the United States, almost all children who have been kidnapped maintain that it was "a black man" who took them away, even in cases where the kidnapper, when discovered, turns out to be white. In France, women who are assaulted sexually often maintain that the perpetrator was an Arab. When the attacker is found, we find that the spontaneous verbal reaction is not always accurate.

Little Bernard had a very clear memory of his escape in 1944 during the transfer to Drancy, the detention camp for Jews: an ambulance at some distance from the row of German soldiers, the end of the process of boarding the sealed railway cars, running through the ranks of soldiers and French military police and disrupting the barricade leading toward the train, a nurse signaling him, the dive under the mattress in the ambulance, a woman dying on the mattress, a German officer giving the sign for departure.

Throughout his life, Bernard kept the memory of the young nurse, a pretty blonde who looked elegant in her uniform. Sixty years later, he happened to find this woman again. At 84 she was still vivacious and pretty. Their recollections were the same in a great many cases, but not entirely. It wasn't an ambulance but a van. The German officer hadn't given the sign for departure, but, on the contrary, had nearly caused the escape to fail. And when Bernard expressed surprise that the woman had dyed her hair black, she did not reply but left the room, returning with a photo: "I was 24," she said. And Bernard saw a young nurse, pretty and elegant in her uniform, with raven-black hair.

It is probably the cultural stereotypes of the time that had retouched Bernard's otherwise very clear memories. When a nurse beckons to you to hide in a car, the logical inference is that it is an ambulance. When an officer gives the signal for departure that means you will not die, his gesture proves that there is always a bit of goodness even in the most wicked human being. And when a woman is pretty, she can only be a blonde in a culture in which American films show goddesses with platinum curls.

Nowadays experimentation and clinical data have given us a better understanding of the way in which a traumatic memory forms. In the earliest months before images and speech, a sensory rupture imbues memory with a selective preference, a trace without recollections. Very soon precise images surrounded by fog form the hard kernel of traumatic memory. And, finally, speech retouches these images so that they can be shared in a social context. The words of the adults in the child's surroundings suggest some interpretative versions, and social discourse, the stereotypes that structure what we say, modifies the memory images so as to make them coherent. What the child says is accurate, but what is said about the child can alter the child's words. Sometimes adults even encourage the child to invent or agree to what sounds plausible, to the detriment of what the child actually intends.[48]

This is why allegations of incest in the course of a request for divorce have a serious psychological effect on a child. The evaluation isn't easy to make, but, whatever the number, there are many such cases. In 25 percent of divorces the mother states that the father has had incestuous relations with children of whom she wants custody.[49] Even when the accusation is ambiguous, the mere reference can be destructive. In 50 percent of divorces, when a mother suggests that some odd behavior may have occurred between her husband and her child, the investigator is sometimes obliged to ask obscene questions in order to get clear answers.[50] Such a process alters the child's memories and behavior and even his affection for his father, who, from then on, will be viewed with fear or disgust.

Children must be protected from real acts of aggression. They must also be protected from allusions. The image memories of small children are reliable, but what adults say can change the way these memories are expressed.[51] The older the child gets, the closer he comes to the linguistic world of adults, and he himself may in turn make use of false allegations in the future.

17. School Reveals a Culture's Idea of Childhood

Thus the child has accumulated a considerable fund of information by
the time he has to face the first major social test of his life: school. On
the first day of school his temperament has already been shaped by early
attachment experiences that have taught him the preferred emotional
and behavioral responses. This special memory is very soon joined by
visual recollections like a silent film. What his parents say, their prejudices, laughter, applause, or threats add another kind of meaning-laden
memory. The child entering school begins to escape parental influence
and come under that of an institution that molds children much more
than one might think.

The entire history of education is, in fact, simply the chronicle of a
culture's ideas of childhood. In ancient Greece, school was above all a
way to shape gestures so as to make social class recognizable. Roman
schools primarily taught rhetoric, and sexual problems were discussed
at length. A woman who had been raped could have her attacker sen-
tenced to two very serious punishments: to die or to marry her. "Knowing that a man can rape two women in a single night, and that one will
condemn him to death, the other to marriage, explain how the judge will
rule."[52]

Elegance of gesture and the handling of language already served to
teach children social distinctions. One was recognized by the flourish
of a hand gesture or the turn of a phrase. Duties and benefits were assigned accordingly, and all that remained was to learn one's trade. The
student discovered mythology that wasn't believed in, but the recitation
of scenes from tragedy and the family relationships among the heroes on
Mount Parnassus were the signposts of belonging to the educated class.

The hand was associated with the tongue in the gestures of eloquence
structuring groups up to the twentieth century. Coeducation did not
prevent gender differences in instruction. Girls excelled in bonds of
solidarity and boys in learning the rituals of civility. In Molière's *School
for Wives*, Arnolphe wants his ward Agnès, whom he wishes to marry
(a common practice in the seventeenth century), to study "the marriage

maxims." In this period, the primary purpose of school was to teach conformity. Personalities had to be adorned in such a way that society could be classified into beautiful souls and rustic minds.

A reconceptualization of the child is an excellent indication that a culture is changing. When little ones are brought up by village clans, kinship notions are not very important, since the child belongs to the group. But when Italian cities were developed, in the Renaissance, the parental home adapted to this new urbanism: the woman at home, the man out in society, and the child with the nanny (if the father could afford one). This personalization of the child highlighted the importance of his emotional life. Some, like Locke in the seventeenth century, wanted to respect it, but many fought against it on the grounds that the emotions debased a man. Physicians stressed that, when boys stopped wearing dresses and put on knee breeches around the age of 7, they began to disdain their parents. And good Dr. Jacques Duval campaigned against the "monkey love" that consisted in hugging one's child so closely that it nearly suffocated.[53]

It was at this time that school stopped being fun, becoming instead a gloomy, confined space where useless information was taught. Physical punishment was not considered violent, because it was educational, even moral. Whippings, spankings, and beatings were in accordance with the cultural stereotype that boys needed to be brought into line in order to make men of them.

Children were taught to endure the brutality of adults. And yet firm bonds of friendship were formed among children educated in this dismal pedagogy.[54] In the few minutes when they escaped their instructors, during games, when school let out, or in the bathrooms, children talked, wove connections, and had an effect on one another, educating themselves in spite of their educators.

One of the most important phenomena of the twentieth century is the expansion of schooling. At the time of Jules Ferry, children entered school at around age 7 and most of them left when they were around 12. Now, at the beginning of the twenty-first century, almost all 3-year-olds are already in school, and they will not leave before they are 25 or 30! A third of one's lifetime, the period when learning takes place most rapidly, is spent at school desks. How can that not have an influence?

The types of pressures that shape our children change whenever the culture changes. In a culture that has discovered the importance of affection, parents want to lead their own lives at the same time. Hence they overinvest signs of affection during the hours that are still available. Parental upbringing, which no longer sees training as a moral method, has transferred its authority to the school and the state. But the attachments that are formed most easily in these strictly operational institutions are insecure, centered on function more than on relationship.

The growth of technology calls for the correct manipulation of abstract knowledge. Only two generations ago, a child who failed in school still held onto his dignity and won his share of happiness by becoming a worker or a farmer. But for some years now a person without a diploma runs the risk of being ostracized from society and humiliated.

18. By the Time a Child Enters School, He Has Already Acquired an Affective Style and Learned His Parents' Prejudices

Emotional socialization is characterized by a relational skill, a way of expressing oneself and forming ties that are less and less codified by cultural rituals. A child who has acquired the relational style of secure attachment will benefit all his life from this learning,[55] whereas a child who has gotten off to a bad start in life because of individual, familial, or social problems will derive less benefit from the support of social codes: "Say hello to the lady. Take off your cap." This was, of course, simply an old-fashioned convention, but it socialized the child better than a repulsive grunt from a child who feels rejected because he hasn't been taught to say hello.

In two generations we have revolutionized the human condition. Ninety percent of all technological and scientific discoveries since the origin of man have been made in the past fifty years. This triumph of abstract knowledge has created a virtual world, a new planet to which we have brought our children with no idea of how they would grow up there.

Bond, function, and meaning (loving, working, and historicizing): these three conditions of a human life have changed. Bonds are increasingly formed outside the family or the village clan. We learn to love in cold institutions where the idolatry of performance contradicts the pious doctrine of egalitarianism: "He got his MBA. She's the champion of the 400-meter hurdle. We are all equal."

I am familiar with the period when people were socialized through the body. A man had to be strong and never complain. A woman had to be a homemaker. Nowadays, men's backs and women's bellies are no longer what socialize us: it is the diploma. This is the new context in which damaged children will have to be mended. In a culture of performance and bulimia, school will have to continue to be a resilience factor.

School and family aren't separate things. The children who make the best adjustment to school are those who have acquired a secure attachment in their families. Conversely, success or failure in school alter the atmosphere at home and the direction of the child's social path. School is not an angelic institution, of course, and it treats the sexes quite differently.

Do you know any children who say, "I go to school in order to learn"? The answers are clear: 60 percent of girls say, "I go to school for Mommy and Daddy." Seventy percent of boys, on the other hand, say, "I go to school for my pals." When invited to explain, the girls add, "I also go there for the teacher." On the whole, children go to school for relational or affective reasons, girls to please adults and boys to meet friends and share activities with them. Only 1 percent of girls and boys go to school to learn!

Failure, too, has a different meaning for each sex. Girls adjust to failure by "acting like a baby" in order to get someone to take charge of them, while boys tend to repair their self-esteem through antisocial conduct or aggression. But siblings, friends, the neighborhood, and even the teacher's personality also play a role in changing the pupil's familial and social directions.[56]

We break things into fragments in order to study them better, but reality is continuous. By viewing school in the context of the family, sexuality, and society, we can understand how it can bring about resilience. The theory according to which school is the primary tool of social reproduction has held true since ancient Greece. This instrument can function effectively even if it transmits no useful knowledge. It is in the margins that we find unexpected ideas that enable us to analyze the process of resilience.

When we study the long-term development of children of the mentally ill, alcoholics, criminals, or sexual aggressors, we find that, twenty years later, when only one parent is affected 25 percent of the children suffer from depression, 75 percent in the case of both parents.[57] This is a much higher rate than in the general population, but this observation helps us understand that almost all of the children who have been able to overcome this emotional and social handicap have found a second circle of close relationships: uncles, cousins, or neighbors willing to serve as substitute support figures.

19. Some Bastion Families Resist Cultural Despair

In societies devastated by war, economic breakdown, and the loss of cultural rituals, most children have difficulty growing up. The exception are children who live in homes with a characteristic structure. Even amid great misery, we find children who do well in school and get a diploma that enables them to pull through. In almost all such cases the family milieu is highly structured: the gestures of affection, the household routines, the religious or secular rituals, and the parental roles are clear. The family members chat a lot, touch one another with gestures and words, share in the upkeep of the household, pray, and tell stories to give meaning to what is going on. The parents form a united front but have differentiated roles.[58]

Such families escape the social effects of their ruined environment. They believe in a space of personal freedom[59]: "It's always possible to make your way in life. Look at your big brother, who came from Italy and had to sleep outdoors for three months. Today he runs his own business." This family belief in internal control creates the equivalent of secure attachment, an inner force that allows the child to escape the stereotypes of his social group.

The Charpaks are the perfect example of these "bastion families" that are poor but reassuring and enlivening: "My parents, I think, had a certain natural refinement. But that was often the case in the working class, where parents made it a point of honor to have polite, helpful, courteous, and respectful children. This respect due our parents went without saying and made us feel very secure, since we knew exactly what the limits were that we couldn't go beyond."[60]

The Charpaks, Jewish immigrants from the Ukraine, settled in Paris. All four of them lived in a small maid's room. The mother worked at home as a seamstress, sewing almost all night long on an old Singer machine. The children slept on a mattress on the floor, and the father got up very early in the morning to make deliveries on a tricycle. But they all had the conviction that work would bring them a better life someday. What was important in this poor family was to keep the children in school. Some years later, despite having been deported to Dachau, Georges passed the entrance exam for the School of Mines and began a career as a physicist that was crowned with a Nobel Prize for France in 1990.

Though uprooted by immigration and resettling, poor families like this see to it that their children fit in from the first generation on and direct them toward advanced technological studies.[61] Practically all these families are "functionalist"; that is to say, each element of the family system adapts to the others so as to accomplish a joint endeavor. This is not a sacrifice but a consecration, since each individual's renunciation of a small, immediate pleasure brings a great deal of happiness to the family as a whole when their dreams are realized. The fathers are authoritarian, the mothers work, and, poverty notwithstanding, the children glorify their parents' courage.

These families function and are organized around giving. Each member knows what the other gives: work, time, affection, and presents. Even the children take part in household tasks. When they happen to earn a little money, they give part of it to their parents. They invest scholastic success with the magical power of healing the parents' trauma: "Of course you suffered by tearing yourselves away from your country of origin and working eighteen hours a day, but your suffering was worth it, since, thanks to you, I'm going to have a wonderful life." This urgent need for success is a happiness poised on a razor's edge, a stimulant bordering on anxiety, insofar as failure would bring a twofold unhappiness.

Amin sold shirts in the flea market at Argenteuil. When the weather was mild it was very pleasant to set up his stand along the Seine, early Sunday morning, near the bridge painted so often by Monet. But Amin annoyed me because, a medical student like myself, he would talk to me by shouting from one stand to the other. In the flea market he would ask me how the anatomy exam had gone, but in the medical school, like every good businessman, he'd be in despair over how little he was earning. I didn't like this way of disengaging from the social setting that welcomed us, even though I understood that, for him, this was a process of finding an identity.

Before the student rebellion of May 1968, the senior members of the medical faculty behaved like aristocrats of the diploma, princes of intellect floating above the vile populace. One Monday morning, Professor Daub questioned my pal from the flea market in front of a lecture hall filled with two hundred students who could not have cared less. That Sunday had been a really tough day, icy, wet, and windy, and Amin hadn't had the strength to prepare the medical assignment. Irritated by his mediocre response, the professor asked,

"What do your parents do?"

"My father is dead, and my mother cleans houses."

The princely professor was virtuously indignant and immediately undertook a lesson in ethics before the now interested students. He explained to my friend that he was acting like a pimp by making his poor mother work and should help her out by dropping his studies. Today Amin is a radiologist, and his mother is happy to have given him so much. Her efforts have taken on meaning, and my pal from the flea market has given her reason to be proud.

"Those who don't know how to give don't know what they're missing,"[62] but a gift has value only in terms of its intention. It may mean an intention to humiliate or to put the other person in our debt, as well as a need to redeem ourselves or a wish to make someone happy. But this little scenario that comes from deep within us takes on different meanings according to its social context.

20. When Street Children Resist Cultural Onslaughts

The World Health Organization and UNICEF estimate that, today, over 100 million children have been put out on the streets. For the most part these are boys between 6 and 17, poorly educated, the products of large families from which the father has disappeared.[63]

Yet within this enormous population we can make out a small group of street children belonging to a kind of family whose emotional organization and ritualized behavior are strongly reminiscent of those poverty-stricken working-class families that, as we have seen, send their children on to careers as nurses, engineers, lawyers, and soldiers. As with my friend from the flea market, the experience of living on the streets has made these children stronger. But if they hadn't had a surrounding emotional envelope and ritual structures, the ordeal of the streets would have shattered them. They would have used toxic substances to help them bear their tribulations; turned to prostitution to earn a living; fallen ill and been rejected, abandoned, beaten, and raped; and, going further and further downhill, they would have become alienated from society. This is what happens to most of them. What causes the collapse, however, is not the assaults but the absence of the social and emotional underpinnings that support resilience.

Michel Le Bris, founder of the "Astounding Voyagers" festival in Saint-Malo and son of an unwed mother, experienced poverty and social stigmatization. Fifty years ago being an unwed mother was considered a grievous fault, but little Michel was not poor when it came to his emotional life. The secure attachment imbued in him by his mother's love gave him a taste for exploration.

Le Bris said he had three strokes of good luck in his life: an elementary-school teacher who introduced him to literature, a high-school teacher who sent him to school in Paris, and the student uprisings of May 1968, which gave him the courage to speak out. But it takes talent to benefit from this so much good luck, and his ability to reach out to others and take pleasure in getting to know them came from the affection his mother gave him, which enabled him to turn misfortune into creativity and the desire to excel.[64] What could have been disgrace became a need to bestow a little pride on the woman who was able to love him despite her difficulties.

Jean-Paul Sartre and Romain Gary made use of the same defensive system, enhancing the prestige of the mother who gave them strength through her love. This is what my friend from the flea market should have explained to Professor Daub. His mother's social vulnerability did not entail a lack of affection, and the child overcame poverty and the disdain of society with the wish to repair the injustice.

It is not only poor or socially vulnerable parents who can provide the love their children need in order to flourish. Even deceased parents can still offer their child a sense of valued identity when they are praised by the culture or have their story told through photos, medals, or other significant objects. On the other hand, some solid parents who have turned out well use their diplomas to appease their insatiable hunger for social success. Despite their fine personal qualities and comfortable surroundings, they don't provide their children with a basis for security. Absent from the home, they do not leave an imprint in the little one's memory. A society that attaches so much value to academic degrees and encourages consumerism creates a thin emotional environment for the child, who will be influenced by people other than the parents. Nowadays it is school that, unintentionally, acts as this substitute.

21. Insufficient Attention Has Been Paid to the Shaping Power of Children Among Themselves

While we can't call it a trauma, we can certainly speak in terms of a major struggle when we note that, in the weeks after a 6-year-old starts school, one out of every two children exhibits behavioral distress: problems with eating and sleeping, nightmares, anxiety, general slowing down, and irritability.

No sooner have these children gotten a basis for security (Mommy, Daddy, the home, the routines) than they are left in a new world with an unfamiliar teacher who has twenty other children to take care of and schoolmates with whom they have to compete in an austere, confined space. If parents are running off to work and leisure activities, or the so-called extended family is shrinking so that it offers only the intermittent presence of one adult, all the child will have in the way of important contacts will be other children in his sibling group or in school, often those who are older. From now on, he will receive their imprints. He is only 6 years old, but already the shaping power of adults is fading.

As for the new people in charge, they are distant figures, unreassuring because they have the power to punish and make rules without emotional involvement. When the child has acquired a serene attachment pattern that lets him enjoy exploration, a new adult figure opens out his mental world. But when a family misfortune or problem has made this type of acquisition precarious, the child experiences the unfamiliar adult as a persecutor to whom he must submit. So he secretly dreams that one day he will rebel. His world splits the way it does after a trauma, dividing into familiar adults who can be dominated because they love the child and unfamiliar adults who can dominate because they are protected by the absence of affection. A social structure categorizing the world in this way can lead to a sense of inner division: the child practices relationships of domination in which people who have the bad luck to feel love are lost, while those who fight against affection feel in control and safe. He does not know that he will have to pay a very high price later on for this ban on loving.

Fortunately, though, in such a social context little ones learn to attach themselves to other children with whom they can get to know different ways of loving. The "big kids" can serve as supports of resilience,
unlike overwhelmed parents and distant teachers. This shaping power
among children has definitely been underestimated in our culture.

The environment molding our children had changed a great deal since
the role of school has expanded. Mothers, increasingly taking part in the
larger world, become imaginary, and fathers are no longer distant, rather
frightening heroes. The extended family has shrunk into separate households, and clans are an empty shell offering only a single model of development. School, on the other hand, along with the neighborhood and the
child's schoolmates, provide young people with the primary opportunities for meeting people and the routines that support development.

All this gives rise to a culture in which children are not shaped by
their families but are abandoned to the influence of adults who manipulate them from the shadows, turning them into playthings for the mar-
ketplace and easy prey for ideologues. This child culture shares some
of the values of the life of street children. Continuous partying becomes
necessary in order to combat despair, the search for intense forms of
stimulation counters the lifelessness of boredom, and risky behavior
creates events that confirm a sense of identity.

In this way our technological culture has brought about a situation
like the one described in *Lord of the Flies*,[65] where the sociologist and
novelist William Golding presciently shows how a group of children
who lack the imprinting of adults reinvent the archaic process of the
constitution of all societies. After a shipwreck near a small island, the
lifeboats containing the adults capsize, and only the children make it to
shore. Gradually, in survival conditions like those of Robinson Crusoe,
two social forms arise: the predators group themselves around a leader
whose power they augment, and the democrats try to organize their
social life.

This is similar to Raphaël's situation in France during the 1950s. His
family had been slaughtered in World War II, and for several years

Raphaël had alternated between periods of dangerous life in the streets and periods of residence in some twenty dreary institutions from which he escaped on a regular basis. One rather warm foster family took him in. But this modern business couple spent their time either working hard or taking well-deserved breaks for winter sports or cruises.

From the age of 12 on, therefore, Raphaël had to run a household without adults. He would get up very early, tidy up, prepare meals for the couple's children, and take them to the babysitter before going off to school. In the evening he would do the shopping on his way back, make dinner, and help the little ones wash up before sitting down to his homework. When the foster parents were present, one or two nights a week, Raphaël would go walking in the old harbor district, where he hung out and watched the people going by.

This is how he made the acquaintance of a small group of teenagers with strong personalities. There was Michel the liar, who sold stolen official documents; cute Alain, who sold his body at elegant evening parties; Alfonso the runt, who laughingly described getting beaten up in fights he himself started; and brainy Eric, who learnedly explained why it was moral to steal from supermarkets.

One evening, when Raphaël had let himself be persuaded of the virtuous necessity of such thefts, he was caught stealing a packet of pens that he didn't need. His life was thrown into disarray. But, surprised by his psychological maturity, and having determined that there was no one at home and that the young thief had to pick up the two children and take care of them that evening, the police let him go.

Several days later, after taking the little ones to the babysitter, instead of heading for school Raphaël got involved in a discussion with the sitter's husband, who was the caricature of what used to be called "an old Communist." This man, a welder with a ready tongue, blithely recited the clichés of his milieu. Raphaël was enchanted by this fluid account, in which the examples were presented with great clarity because they had been so often repeated. The next evening, at a café, he drew his little gang into a political discussion. All of them were filled with enthusiasm except cute Alain, who found all this ridiculous and far less lucrative than sex parties in rich neighborhoods.

The group changed its tone. The boys bought the leftist newspaper *L'Humanité*, commenting on the headlines so as to find reasons to get indignant. Eric was convinced that petty theft was not the way to fight the big supermarkets. Alain scornfully decided not to have anything more to do with this gang of losers. But Raphaël was surprised by how intensely happy these new discussions made him.

This process, a frequent occurrence in our Western culture, is similar to what happens with street children. The adult is there, to be sure, but not as a support. A child adrift is usually easy prey for the purveyors of sex, exploitative labor, or extreme ideologies.

22. A Silent but Deeply Meaningful Encounter Can Bring About Resilience

When a child drifts too close to a predator, merely holding out a helping hand to him can bring rescue. Even an ordinary chat can be an event that changes the course of his life. This is often the case when teachers are effective, just as much as through the abstract knowledge they transmit. They become supports of resilience for a wounded child when they bring about an event that takes on the significance of a landmark.

Miguel's father was a journalist in Santiago. He had to flee one night, just before the militia arrived, but he was arrested the next day at the home of friends. Only Miguel and his mother were able to get on a plane to Paris.

Soon thereafter, the mother fell sick and died, leaving her 16-year-old son alone with incomplete identification papers and a language in which he wasn't fluent. For this boy, school became his main hope for integration into his new society. He worked as a window washer early in the morning, after which he would jump on his bike and ride to his high school. Even before the first class began, he had three hours of work behind him. At noon he worked as a waiter in a cafeteria before going back to class in the afternoon.

Mr. Bonnafe, who taught biology, had a reputation for strictness. Yet he never raised his voice, preferring to hold a supply of little pieces of chalk in his left hand and throw them right at the heads of students who gossiped or were inattentive. No one protested, though an anxious silence loomed over the class.

One day Bonnafe came for lunch to the cafeteria where Miguel was waiting tables. Not a word was exchanged, but the teacher's long, intent gaze gave Miguel to understand that an event had taken place. That afternoon, in class, the boy sensed a slight raising of the teacher's eyebrows and an imperceptible nod of his head that definitely meant, "I take my hat off to you."

This tiny sign was the beginning of a special relationship. From then on, the teacher kept an eye on Miguel, returning homework assignments to him silently and occasionally seeming to speak directly to him in class. This mute complicity made the boy markedly sensitive to the natural sciences. He did his work carefully, knowing that Bonnafe attached importance to whatever he handed in. He made great progress, putting so much effort into this material that, some years later, he became a doctor.

We can't say that it was a teacher's raised eyebrows that made this boy a doctor, since even in Chile he had dreamed of this career. But what is true is that a child puts effort into an area of study only for someone else's sake. The slightest significant gesture conveying the idea "You exist in my mind, and what you do matters to me" illuminates a piece of the world and heightens awareness of a form of abstract knowledge. The resilience effect occurred thanks to a mute but deeply meaningful encounter in which the man and the boy became important to one another. For Bonnafe, the child meant: "He is braver than I was when I had to interrupt my studies," and, for the boy, the teacher meant: "I've gained his respect, and so I'm worthy of respect even though I'm physically exhausted and poor."

It is astonishing to note the extent to which teachers underestimate their influence as people and overestimate their transmission of knowledge. Many, many people tell their therapists how much a teacher changed their lives, years ago, simply through an attitude or a few words, ordinary for the adult but decisive for the child.

Teachers aren't aware of this power. Asked about their students' academic success, they almost never attribute it to their own influence.[66] Instead, they speak of qualities inherent in the student: "He had a good head on his shoulders," "She was able to absorb the material," "He was studious"—as though the child had some sort of scholastic aptitude apart from his or her teachers, a fertile field in which the knowledge implanted in it could grow.

For a damaged child, the hunger for understanding grows in the form of a constructive defense, intellectualization. Mathematics, which provides immense understanding of the universe, is not of much help in such a defense unless it enhances self-esteem. In that case, it is the success that produces the effect of a defense more than the pleasure taken in comprehending. In contrast, the social sciences and humanities (politics, literature) not only lend coherence to the child's shattered world but also bring about a feeling of calmness that enables him to adopt a form of conduct he can maintain, a manner of governing his inner life.

This reasoning holds for teachers who feel undermined when their student's failure seems to reflect on the instructor's shortcomings. They behave toward the children in such a way as to reveal their own disorganization. "Miguel, you're late again. You're dozing off. Your attempts to explain the material are clumsy." We can imagine that Mr. Bonnafe felt something of this kind before he saw Miguel scrambling among the cafeteria tables to earn his meager salary. In a single episode the teacher went from irritation to respect, changing his inner conceptual world.

This is why teachers who believe in resilience bring it about much more readily than those who don't. Even if they haven't thought the notion through, the mere conviction forms an inner representation that is expressed in ways that the child perceives as enormously important and clear.

This is not a behavioral recipe, however. A support for resilience calls for a constellation of pressures. The slight interpersonal change signaling the conceptual change in the teacher's mind is better accepted by girls, more readily transformed by them into a support for resilience, since from the beginning they have gone to school to please Mom, Dad, and the teacher. In contrast, many boys fail to form such a support because, in contexts where peer pressure repudiates school, such signs do not mean much.

23. We Can Overinvest in School in Order to Please Our Parents or Escape Them

When my friend Abel Raledjian decided to go to medical school in Marseilles, his family was ecstatic. Yet they lived in poverty, selling pants in the Rue du Baigneur near the old port. When he was not in school, the boy helped his parents by doing alterations and making deliveries. He had a lot of friends in the nearby shops that sold hardware, pastries, and household appliances. The day he announced his intention to study medicine, he delighted his family and lost his friends: "Only girls and fags like to study. A real man is a laborer like us."

In the minds of his friends, he had betrayed them by venturing into the middle class, but for his parents his decision gave their sacrifice a meaning. If Abel had chosen to share his friends' world, he wouldn't have noticed the signs of encouragement his teachers were giving him, signs to which he became highly sensitive once he decided to follow the path approved by his family. One and the same act took on different meanings according to the cultural and emotional context: "You're betraying us" versus "You're doing us proud."

Academic support for resilience can sometimes come at a price. Marina's father had fled Fascist Italy at eleven o'clock one night. He had gone to the station and told the ticket seller, "I want to go to France. Give me the ticket I can buy with the money I have on me." This is how he got to La Ciotat, where he got off the train into a country and language he didn't know.

Having found a hovel in a vineyard, he was hired by the owner. Marina was born there and spent her childhood ashamed of having parents who were uneducated and poor. Her dress was dirty and she had no shoes, but her suffering was eased when she dreamed of her shame disappearing the day she would become a teacher of French.

And that is what she became. But she fulfilled this resilient dream only by dint of fighting with her father every day. For him, the courage to survive came through physical effort. When he saw his daughter reading, he became irate and started kicking her books, the furniture, and sometimes the child herself. How dare she take time off to read, an idle pleasure, when he had to struggle to survive and establish his place in his new country. Marina's dream of resilience was proof of laziness to her father. So she studied in secret in order to redress her shame, sad not to be able to share this pleasure with her father.

Once again it was a teacher who encouraged Marina's process of resilience by asking her to write about the way she pictured the country of her origin. The child wrote a lovely description of the beauty of Italy, placing there a nice father who, though he came from a humble background, was highly educated. She reread this account over and over again, keeping it carefully hidden while dreaming of her father discovering it, reading it, and becoming a changed man.

Finally, we can find a common element among poor families who bring up their children for academic success and students who, despite their families, blossom in school: both believe in a kind of inner freedom, as though to say, "I don't see why I should submit to the statistics claiming that a child of the working class won't go on to higher education," or "I don't see why I should hate reading the way my father would like me to." This internal control[67] is costly, since the latter type of family is often isolated from its social context. Sometimes it is even the child who has to separate himself, study in secret, and lose the respect of those close to him.

24. Belief in One's Dreams as Inner Freedom

The feeling of inner freedom, of a capacity for self-determination, is acquired early on, probably at the time of the imprinting of secure attachment. If there is aggression, the child continues to believe in his choices and his dreams, not just in stimuli coming from without. He is less context-dependent, forging his way in accordance with his inner world.

Nadir was having trouble with his legal studies. Not only did he have to earn a living at the same time as he was going to law school, but he could not even talk about this at home because his family resented his academic success. His father, who dreamed of becoming a real Frenchman, had joined the *harkis*, Algerian soldiers who fought on the French side during the war of independence. When Algeria won its independence, he had to flee to a hut on the seacoast.

Nadir wasn't his mother's favorite. She was more comfortable with her daughters, who laughed all the time as they went about their household chores, and with her other sons, whom she considered less pretentious than Nadir with his complicated way of expressing himself.

When Nadir was in his second year of law school, a professor announced the results of the written exam out loud before calling the candidates to present themselves for the oral exam. Like everyone else, Nadir waited for his name to be called, but next to him another candidate was trying to make his neighbors laugh by adding, "Died for France" each time a foreign name was uttered. "Sami Idrir"—"Died for France." "Angelo Francesco"—"Died for France." "Jacques Lebensbaum"—"Died for France." "Nadir Belchir"—"Died for France."

For a brief moment Nadir indulged the fantasy of punching him in the face. He was bigger than this young man and would have crushed him. And yet . . . might he also break his glasses, or might the uproar of the fight prevent him from working? Nadir said nothing and was not proud of this, but he thought to himself, "What matters is to fulfill my plans. If I responded to this guy I'd be submitting to his world and would lose some of my freedom." Two minutes later Nadir calmly went back to work.

Here we see what is so often the case in abusive families. In half of such families, only one child becomes the target for mistreatment, while in the other half all the children are beaten. Some children physically confront the violent parent, but others escape by drawing into themselves: "Poor Mom, you're not a grown-up when you hit me like that. You're letting your impulses get the better of you."

Twenty years later, the children who fought back do not do well. They have adapted themselves to the abusive context, and their behavioral response has subjected them to it. In contrast, the abused children who escaped inside themselves were unhappy, but later on they were able to realize part of their dreams and thereby mend their damaged self-esteem.

What counts is the meaning of school or the intellectual adventure for them. The meaning of an object does not lie in that object but in what the milieu attributes to it. Samira was a truly difficult girl. She always came late to school and provoked the teacher. Any form of authority aroused her rebellion. She was proud of this and made it part of her identity. One evening, going off with a boy she was fond of, she was raped in a club set up for this purpose. Stunned, she told her parents everything, and they threw her out of the house.

And so she became a "club girl," damned by her family and scorned by the boys and girls in her neighborhood. But a surprising thing happened in the midst of her growing despair: school took on a different meaning. It was the only place where people spoke kindly to her. "I cling to school," she said, "because at least I have a stable setting."[68] Before the trauma, school had been a constraining prison that she had to oppose. Afterward, the same setting became reassuring and made it possible for her to find some hope. Samira was able to take advantage of this, for today she has her diploma, lives surrounded by friends, and works in a cultural institute.

Obviously, we must not traumatize children to get them to like school, but we may suggest that a set of converging forces is what gives school its meaning. Samira was saved by the school she had earlier attacked because, after her trauma, the establishment became a haven of kindness for her, a hope for finding freedom. In a wretched environment she was able to make a small island of beauty for herself.

Not all children are protected by school, and some are even damaged there. A teacher can bring about a metamorphosis in a child with a simple word or a sustained gaze. (*Metamorphosis* means a change of form, not necessarily an improvement.)

When an abused child enters school, he has almost always acquired an insecure attachment, and this way of dealing with relationships marginalizes him. When he arrives, he does not make overtures to the other children, and when he is invited in by them he avoids the encounter. Unhappy, lacking self-confidence, he stands on the periphery, doesn't make eye contact, sucks his thumb, rocks back and forth, or feigns interest in something off to one side so that he doesn't have to look straight at others.[69]

This behavioral style attracts the attention of another type of child: the bully. There were always bullies in schools, but there were fewer of them and you could always run away or protect yourself from them. Nowadays, it would seem, children who are abused at home give the impression of being easy prey. The way in which abused children defend themselves against bullies is a reliable predictor of later problems.[70]

A small percentage of abused children fight back against the bullies at school. In the short run they're proud of the physical confrontation that allows them to think, "I was brave. I stood up to him. No one is going to pick on *me* like that." This behavioral scenario gives the child a certain sense of worthiness despite everything.

The child bully, too, is almost always unhappy at home. He adds luster to his tarnished self-image by convincing himself that his physical strength inspires terror. The child who, despite his relative weakness, stands up to him is adopting a similar strategy for gaining a sense of self-worth.

Both of these groups are headed for academic failure and desocialization. The immediate benefit of the triumph does not have time to sink in. Quite the contrary: the non-belligerent children move away and abandon them to their alienating defense mechanism. The surprise comes when we follow these groups over time. Most of the children who are abused at home and let themselves be bullied at school evolve toward a long, secret depression in which they suffer pain. But it is in this population that we later find the largest number of resilient people!

The bullied children who adopted the same defensive style as the bullies benefit only in the short run. Then they always have to begin all over again. Violent children are surrounded and admired by a group of subordinate leaders, but this doesn't keep them from being rejected. This toxic defense mechanism shows that such children almost always suffer from problems of attachment,[71] and the morbid duo drag one another toward desocialization. In contrast, the group of silent depressives and secret sufferers form constructive defenses: daydreaming, intellectualization, activism, anticipation, and sublimation. If an adult is willing to act as a support for resilience in order to mobilize their hidden abilities, these children will come back to life to the point where the silent depression will give way under the influence of emotional, intellectual, and social efforts.

25. A Defense That Is Legitimate but Cut Off from Others Can Become Toxic

When children are abandoned to their mute suffering, however, many of them will be destroyed by their own defense mechanisms.[72] The denial that protects them condemns them to silence. The daydreaming that creates an inner world of beauty may cut them off from the social world. Their fear of others leads to increased absenteeism. Often a maladaptive intellectualization makes these children seem dull in school, whereas in fact they are actually very well versed in a marginal area.

When we allow the bullied to get rejected, when we neglect the secret depression of the abused, these children learn despair and the masking of pain. But when we help them make use of what their suffering has set in place, many of them will become resilient.

What we have come to see in the past few years is that mutual shaping also occurs among siblings.[73] Often it is an older brother or sister who sets the behavioral tone. Some older sibs have an aspiring influence that carries the younger children along with it. Identification with an older child can lead to sibling groups of artists, good students, brawlers, or cop-outs. On the other hand, we often find that an older child takes advantage of his strength and authority to establish a relationship of control that, unbeknownst to the parents, may border on sadism. Likewise, a sick child in the family changes the parents' behavior and hence the sensory bubble and support system surrounding the healthy children.

Sylvaine was 5 when her little brother was born with Down syndrome. In less than two months the little girl became serious. She could not understand that the baby was going to develop in a special way, but, as soon as he was born, she no longer had the same parents. Her mother quit her job, and, despite her greater presence at home, she spoke and smiled less to Sylvaine. Since the father was now the only wage earner, he stayed away more often to do extra work, and, when he was home, he too had grown serious and played less with his daughter. So Sylvaine adapted to this new world, and, sensing her parents' vulnerability, she grew up and took charge of them.

Such a child is supported by the gestures, facial expressions, and words of the adults to whom he is attached. He is well aware of his parents' interactions but has not yet attained their values, nor does he have an idea of their social status. But when the meaning of life changes for the parents, the sensory environment in which the child is steeped changes as well.

When children who grow up prematurely are shaped by institutions, we often find two extreme relational styles: the extroverted group who act, speak, and play easily and oppose adults without fear, and the introverted group who are silent, avoidant, or even anxious. When we observe these children for a brief time, we find that the extroverts laugh, move, and speak with ease, whereas the introverts, fearful and marginalized, aren't far from depression. But when we see them again twenty years later, the introverts who didn't do well academically because they were unhappy at home and in school have often compensated for their deficiencies by developing an imagination that has given them the hope and the desire to pull through.[74]

Children can shape one another because they have abilities similar to those of adults: identification with an older sibling and relationships of control or protection of a vulnerable younger child. They can help or hinder one another just as adults do. School can thus be a place of boredom and bad influences as easily as it can be a factor in resilience,[75] depending on the meaning ascribed to it by the community.

An emotional and behavioral tendency in a child can become a stable acquisition if the milieu is stable. But every change in the system alters the tendency and diverts the course of the child's life.

26. School Is a Resilience Factor When the Family and the Culture Give It This Power

A phenomenon illustrating this idea recently occurred in Baltimore. Most of the boys from the black neighborhoods refused to go to school. They influenced one another, evading parental control and filling their days with a delinquent heroism that often landed them in jail.

One day, however, a mother, desperate when she saw her 8-year-old son proudly rebelling against all authority and going in the direction of delinquency, decided to send him to live with a cousin far away, a Masai in Africa. The child returned completely transformed: kind, cooperative, a good student and happy to be one. Today there are two groups in Baltimore: those who stayed in the United States and are still headed toward prison, and those who, after a simple stay in Africa, graduate from high school, learn a trade, and don't complain about it.[76]

Totally different structuring environments attribute contrasting meanings to school. In Baltimore, the only way boys struggle against their isolation is by meeting other boys in the street who disdain school. The only contacts with adults come in the form of threats and repressions. Events and distractions come only from other children evading the police and confronting the world of anonymous adults.

Among the Masai a child is never alone, yet he feels free and protected because the adults teach him how to avoid the dangers surrounding him. In such a context, the adults convey a sense of safety that, early on, gives the child his share of responsibility. Depending on the way the milieu is organized, school can become a source of scorn or of happiness. Teachers and pupils are, of course, also actors within this system.[77]

When our children enter school, 70 percent of them have acquired a secure attachment that makes this major event a game of exploration, a pleasurable discovery. But one out of three insecurely attached children hardly speaks, stays on the periphery, and suffers in silence because he has learned to fear others and feel anxious in the face of the unknown. Almost all insecurely attached children and even some of the securely attached ones have been traumatized. Only one child in two experiences

going to school as an exciting adventure. The day they begin, they have
already acquired a way of loving and learned all the prejudices of their
family. Shaping will occur under the combined influence of siblings and
friends. Children do not necessarily form the strongest attachment to
the teachers with the most credentials, preferring those whose personality makes them feel safe and energized.

Hence the child will have to make his way under the influence of a
whole constellation of determinants as he constructs his resilience. This
is why we can't attribute an effect to a single cause. We can't say that
school destroys a child or saves him. Both can occur. But when aggression comes from outside the family, the supports for resilience come
from within it, as in those "bastion families" that know how to protect
and enliven their children.[78] When aggression occurs within the family, supports for resilience have to be sought in the environment: uncles,
aunts, grandparents, neighbors and neighborhood, school, and cultural
organizations.

Children of miners worshipped their fathers, family heroes sacrificed
on the altar of industry. These men went down into the mines at the age
of 12, knowing that they would practically never see daylight again,
would have to crawl through overheated galleries at risk of accidents,
or would die a slow death suffocating from silicosis. In this technical
and industrial context, in which aggression was extreme, the family
came to represent a protective haven. Though they were hardly ever
at home, the fathers filled the imagination of the families and the culture and became heroes.

27. The Strange Household of the Adultist Child

When aggression is insidious we have difficulty becoming aware of it. And yet its everyday weight structures the child, who learns to adapt to a slow rift.

The children of vulnerable parents cling to their fragile supports and adjust to this milieu very carefully. This is what happens when we walk on a poorly defined mountain path: we pay attention to the fallen rocks, remove loose stones, and push aside branches that could make us lose our balance. The mental and behavioral worlds of the children of vulnerable parents may be called *adultist*. This isn't a good term, but that is why it must be kept: it is unusual and refers to behavior that is simultaneously adaptive and pathological.

When we follow the psychological development of a group of children whose parents are vulnerable because of mental illness, physical handicaps, alcoholism, or incarceration, we find that almost half of them—45 percent—become anxious adults with labile emotions and an inner world often filled with pain, in contrast to 23 percent in the general population. But, several decades later, a good half of the people in this group will have become serene, flourishing adults,[79] albeit at the great cost of the life strategy of adultism.

The 45 percent who became suffering adults were left alone with the vulnerable parent, but the people in the larger half had always been able to find a familial or cultural bond outside their odd household, a bond in which the child didn't have to be a parent to his parents. Surrounding the family that parentified the child were supports for resilience: a school, a youth club, an athletic team, an uncle, a neighbor, or a group of friends allowing the child to exist and develop as a child.

What is it that so often makes the children of immature parents become adults prematurely? Our reference point here can be children whose parents have died. In the orphan's imagination, death has conferred a special status on the deceased parents. These are the only children with parents who are forever young and forever perfect. In contrast, those who are lucky enough to have real parents will inevitably have to deal at some point

with a tired or unfair father or a mother who is irritable or who leaves
her child in favor of some other concern of hers.

The child who has real, and hence imperfect, parents learns to come
to terms with them, enduring their small injustices and abandonments,
which gradually takes him in the direction of autonomy. But the child
of dead, and hence perfect, parents grows up in a split world in which
reality is cruel and imagination wondrous. When they do not break
down, these orphans will become "little grown-ups" in more than half
of the cases. The environment sings their praises, they are said to be
serious and reasonable, and yet they convey an uneasy feeling. Their
way of making contact is too polite, a bit verbose, even mannered.
Their sense of responsibility is impressive but disquieting. Their affected smile keeps us at a distance, their over-refinement makes us
want to shake them, and their charming behavior lacks all charm. We
want to say bad things about them, yet their performances oblige us
to speak well of them.

I recall Antoine, orphaned at an early age and quite retarded mentally
after passing through some fifteen institutions in which he had never had
time to form close ties. At around age 12 he was finally placed with a family and suddenly began to behave quite differently. The couple sold cold
cuts from a truck, and Antoine had to take care of their house and their
children. He looked upon this work with excessive seriousness. In school,
Antoine became a good student, whereas before he had been inhibited,
almost feeble-minded.

Several years later, when it became possible to enter his inner world,
it was clear that this adultism was the socially acceptable form of an
avoidant attachment, as though Antoine had told himself, "I do what I
have to do. They're keeping me in their home, and I'll buy my freedom
by being a perfect child just as my dead parents were perfect. We're
even, so I can leave them someday without remorse." His avoidant attachment, together with his perfect behavior as a foster child, was in fact
a life strategy adapted to his situation. Antoine was buying himself his
future detachment, his freedom down the line.

This adjustment strategy is like an internal over-control, as though the child had said:

> By seeming to submit, I'm buying my freedom. I'm giving up immediate gratification so that later on these people won't keep me from enjoying life by asking me to take care of them. I'm paying in advance. My abnormal docility is a preparation for my detachment. Up to now my reality has been hopeless, but ever since I've been given responsibilities I'm hopeful again as I discover that I can prevail over reality.

This way of repairing self-esteem is costly, but how could one do otherwise?

The adultist child isn't nice so that people will like him. He is not interested in forming a bond, unlike children who have acquired an untroubled attachment. He is nice in order to free himself. But this way of winning autonomy appears only when the parents are of a certain type. In the course of his earlier placements, Antoine had exhibited different kinds of attachment, depending on the foster family. Sometimes he had been dull-witted, distant, and uncommunicative. Other times he had been adorable, industrious, or careful not to be too much of a burden to the family that had taken him in. But what surprised him the most was that, before he was placed with the butchers, he had spent several months with a highly structured family in which the husband and wife, both decorators, had completely inhibited him. Cowed, and feeling distant from this couple whom he admired but couldn't identify with, Antoine didn't dare to do anything at home or in school.

When he came to the butchers, the little boy was astounded by how uneducated they were and quite content with the tasks they heaped on him. The couple who were decorators made him feel ashamed of himself, but the weakness and rough-hewn naïveté of the butchers enabled him to prove himself capable of running a household, taking care of children, and doing well in school.

Adultism makes it possible for the child not to have to depend on others' love: "I rule, I pay, I leave." We may conjecture that, had he stayed with the decorators, Antoine would have sought to gain his autonomy by quickly learning any trade whatsoever as long as it allowed him to leave and never see this nice foster family again. With the butchers, on the other hand, the child overloaded with work began daydreaming once more, deciding to do what his mother had wished for before her death: "My son will be a famous lawyer." And so this is what he asserted violently, almost screaming, when the "daddy" butcher wanted to teach him his trade so that he and his wife could lean on Antoine in their old age. Going to work at an early age would have bound him to the butcher family, while the same early work would have freed him from the decorators. The resilience strategies would have been different, depending on the foster family.

28. Morbid Devotion, the Excessive Offering of Oneself, as the Price of Freedom

It is almost a rule that an immature parent prompts the parentification of one of the children.[80] And it is even thanks to this costly process that children growing up in families where incest is practiced manage to break free and become resilient.

Lorenzo was 14 when he caught his father in bed with his sister. After raging inwardly for several weeks he decided to go to the police. His father was called in. The man was surprised and stunned that he had been informed on. He offered so much evidence of his devotion that it was the son who had to see a psychiatrist and take medication.

Two years later, the sister caught her father with the youngest daughter. This time the combined testimony of the two teenagers sent the father to prison. But Lorenzo had no sense of triumph. On the contrary, he felt guilty about his family's financial collapse: it was his fault that they were poor, his fault that his sisters weren't able to pursue their studies. So he found work as a mason and took care of the household, the domestic chores, and the paperwork while his sisters went to school.

The incestuous parent is not strong, reassuring, and energizing because he has no access to a sense of parenthood. He does not feel like a father and views his daughter as a little wife. Faced with a strong parent, a child affirms himself in opposition. Lorenzo, however, faced with an immature father and a mother who was busy elsewhere, discovered his strength by taking charge of the house and becoming a "father" to his mother and little sisters. The immediate benefit of his adultism was the easing of his guilt and the restoration of his wounded self-esteem as he helped the weak. This costly strategy enabled the child to feel worthy and virtuous once again.

The workings of justice are sometimes surprising. Little Claude's father had killed the mother in the child's presence. The boy didn't say a word when he was placed in a cold institution. The emotional coldness suited him well, since it allowed him to adjust without having to work at human relationships.

After several months of hibernation he was entrusted to an unmarried young aunt, a stripteaser. Since she worked nights and slept during the day, the child grew bored and began to miss the gloomy orphanage. When his aunt decided to become respectable one day, she asked the little boy to choose between two suitors, one a jolly, athletic man Claude liked a lot, the other sad and annoying. He chose the latter because he had one unquestionable advantage: a dislocated hip! Having been made over-responsible by his immature aunt, the child could not inflict an emotional injury on this man. He would suffer less by inflicting the deprivation on himself.

Freedom can't be won with impunity, and, like Lorenzo, Claude worked at becoming a moral little man, preparing for an offering up of self that was morbid in its excessiveness. But if someone offers to satisfy the needs of others at the expense of his own, he is not a member of the Masoch family because he is not using this strategy to seek his own pleasure. He gains self-esteem but not enjoyment: "The athletic one is the one I like, the one who laughs all the time. But I couldn't bear to be a child who does bad things. I'll give up my pleasure"—a masochist would look for it—"so as to make myself into a moral man." This is what Claude might have said.

All we can do is endure reality and adapt to it under penalty of death, but a child doesn't even know what to do to confront it. He needs someone else if he is to learn how to live and to acquire some relational skills that will characterize his emotional style. Thus he may turn out to be difficult or easy to love, enterprising or inhibited. Being an adult means having the skills necessary for satisfying real needs by taking pleasure in their representation. My body needs water (this is reality), and I'll put it in a blue bottle (this is the representation of reality).

"Psychological maturity is the result of a supported mental development."[81] Emphasizing the pathological aspect of the child-adult, Freud had spoken of premature ego development, Ferenczi of the precocious maturity of worm-eaten fruit.[82] It is my impression that the morbidity of adultism is, rather, an adaptation to familial or social pressure. We may wonder why certain families promote immaturity while others foster precocious maturity. It would seem that, when a milieu puts all the constraints of reality in the hands of attachment figures, the child feels stuffed full and can't conceptualize them. He doesn't have to learn relational skills because his reality is already complete. When the milieu supplies everything, the child doesn't realize that he needs water.

An adult needs both the water and the blue bottle. A child who has been stuffed full wants neither of these. A deprived one needs water so much that he couldn't care less about the color of the bottle. This is how disparate environments promote different kinds of development in the way they reconcile reality and the way reality is represented.

29. Extricating Oneself from Sacrifice so as to Gain Autonomy

When the torn child submits to the injury because no one has told him that he could be sewn back together, he suffers psychological trauma. Once started on this path, some children adapt to it, taking charge of all the problems in their small world in a kind of self-centered activity that is, however, directed not toward their own bodies but instead toward their immediate environment.

When trauma befalls an older child, he reacts not so much by rocking back and forth or touching himself all the time the way a small child would, but more by assuming responsibility for those around him. Such conduct may be protective in the short run, but if it goes on too long it becomes a hindrance to personality development. The child must then disengage himself from adultism, giving up this protection so as to become resilient.

This process of resistance-resilience[83] is common when life becomes too much of an uproar. We first have to confront and adapt, whatever the cost. Then, when things settle down, we have to disengage in order to resume our development, making something of the injury by giving it a meaning. Growing up too much and too fast is not an advance; it represents a delay, but after this long detour resilience becomes possible. Acting like an adult enables the wounded child to feel less diminished, but pretending to be a mommy or making decisions like a little man is a dangerous pleasure: this "as if" game teaches the child a role incompatible with his personality. The wounded child, knowing that the performances put on by others are always a kind of language,[84] puts himself onstage as a character. He plays the role of someone eager to leave behind the hardship of being a child. Acting like an adult makes him feel that he is no longer alone. But the little actor is reciting a role he doesn't experience, since he doesn't like being a grown-up and, often, doesn't even like the person to whom he is devoting himself.

One Wednesday afternoon, Nicolas had to miss a soccer match with the junior team of his high school in order to take the children of his foster family for a walk. The boy had put a textbook on top of the stroller and was trying to study while he kept watch over the children when an older couple, charmed by this picture, began to compliment him. Nicolas was surprised by the foul insults that escaped from his mouth. He was quite willing to do housework at five in the morning, miss a soccer game, babysit the children, and study so as to get good grades, but he was furious when labeled "nice." He didn't want to be the kind of person whose role merely afforded him a strategy for freeing himself: "I adapt, I pay, I don't owe anyone anything. This long detour is the only way I can become myself someday."

What else could he do? Nicolas had often seen rebellious boys in orphanages desocializing themselves by running away, stealing, and fighting. Those boys lost their freedom by indulging in a few short moments of self-enhancement: "Did you see what I pulled off when I stole that, how brave I was in the fight?" A brief victory, at too great a cost. For Nicolas, adultism became a tunnel he was gradually digging, bringing himself closer to freedom with each day.

But not always. The adultism that leads to freedom contrasts with the adultism of children who are overattached to a vulnerable parent. Prisoners of the adult's immaturity, they don't dare separate themselves. They are ashamed of freedom, as though it meant abandoning someone close, a child.

Pierre's mother had to work as a nurse to pay for her own medical studies. She was lively, warm, and active but completely incapable of planning her workday. She would forget appointments, lose administrative papers, and go on vacation when her colleagues were waiting for her in a lawyer's office. Pierre learned early on to take her in charge. The child filled the fridge, organized her files, and thought to himself that she should really tell him who his father was.

After graduating from high school he earned money for college by conducting tours; his mother already had incurred many debts. One day she told him, in tears, that she had to give up her broken-down car and as a result would not be able to make her nursing visits the following day. The young man immediately took out a student loan, bought his mother a car, and worked even harder to pay her debts.

Because of his mother's immaturity, Pierre was faced with an impossible choice: when he hovered around her he compromised his own growth, but when he distanced himself in order to work better he was tormented by guilt. Whatever he decided would be painful. But what was striking was the extent to which mothering his mother led to an anxious overattachment in him. We often see the same thing when a mother is taking care of a vulnerable child, one who is ill or difficult. The care offered to the weaker person fosters attachment and lends value to the caregiver.

Adultism is a long detour that can lead to resilience on condition that the child makes use of it to free himself and become responsible for himself. When a child who is too good and too devoted lets himself become the prisoner of the person he is protecting, both parties go under. But when helping an adult has been protective for a child, allowing him to undertake the fulfillment of a personal project, he may be considered ungrateful by the neighbors who formerly admired him but he will be able to resume his own development.

Again, context serves as an orientation point. Bernadette, Eric, and Irène were much more preoccupied with their mother than with their schoolmates. Each of these children had a different father who had disappeared before their birth. The mother lived on welfare and remained in bed, where she would receive a transient lover every now and then. The children took care of everything, spending most of their time comforting their mother, until the day Bernadette fell in love—with a black man. When the affair became serious, she had to introduce him to her mother, who could not keep herself from uttering racist insults. In her anger, she threw her daughter out of the house. Bernadette, very unhappy, was worried about her mother at first and asked her brother and little sister to take care of her. Several weeks later, though, she was very surprised to find how easy life had become.

The academic success of the adultist child is often humiliating to the adult who has been taken in charge by that child. The overly serious child comes across as a schoolmaster. He is rather preachy and condescending as he explains the way the world works. This is annoying, especially when his siblings act like normal children, giggle, do dumb things, and are only intermittently interested in school.

In such cases, the vulnerable parents make a great effort, albeit a nonverbal one, to undermine the child who is helping them. The mother may "forget" to give him the registration fee for an exam. She may "lose" the application form for a scholarship. The immature father may manage to arrive late for the job interview he had promised to attend with his son. The failure scenarios are numerous, varied, and all "accidental," but what they actually show is the wish to put obstacles in the path of this too-nice child, making it harder for him to become autonomous. He has to be kept at home, in the case of anxious overattachments, or made to fail when his success humiliates his immature parents.

For it is, indeed, the gaining of autonomy that leads to resilience. When development is normal, the child gradually separates from the source of attachment that, imprinted in his memory, gives him the strength to leave it. When there has been a trauma, growth in the direction of resilience should do likewise, but, because it involves getting back on track despite a rupture and in adverse circumstances, it calls for costlier strategies.

Starting at age 6, the growing child finds support outside the family, for the most part from the extended family, school, and the neighborhood. If the adultist child finds a pal, a teacher, an athletic coach, or a romantic partner outside the realm of his household, he often undergoes a transformation.

It was a high-school friend who set Antoine on the path toward autonomy, enabling him to get free of the nice but oppressive butchers. Roland was 12, one year older than Antoine. He had achieved secure attachment despite his parents' divorce. The mother, an authoritarian who worked hard, headed a fashion house, while the father, a poet and teacher, devoted his life to organizing delightful get-togethers, Sundays in the country, and fine discussions at the table. These parents couldn't get along with one another, yet they had each left a rich psychological inheritance to Antoine. His strength came from his mother, his sense of beauty from his father.

As soon as he entered high school, Antoine found Roland, whose self-confidence, cheerfulness, and soccer skills he found hugely impressive. The two boys lived in the same district. They went home together after school and bonded in friendship.

Despite his apparent strength, Antoine felt like his parents' child. His mother wanted him to succeed in life, and so he made her supervise his homework. Roland, in turn, was impressed by the apparent maturity of Antoine, who already knew how to run a household. Thanks to this friendship, Antoine was invited to the home of Roland's father, the poet-teacher, where he suddenly felt like a child. He learned to cook, drink fine wines, do silly things, and sing naughty songs in front of the father, who would pretend to be virtuously indignant.

This entire world of make-believe made Antoine truly happy. He found that, with the butchers, he always felt overwhelmed, whereas his friendship with Roland helped him understand that a child has the right to receive guidance. This friendship, of course, could not have come about with just anyone: Antoine was receptive to the kind of person Roland was. He had come across many boys in his neighborhood who talked about nothing but fighting and thievery, but he had never gotten to know them, as had been the case with the antisocial boys in the institutions where he had spent time. When, some years later, Roland enrolled in law school with the aim of studying for the school career his mother dreamed of, Antoine wondered why he was doing so. By serving as a support for resilience, Roland enabled Antoine to head toward autonomy and break free of his childhood devotion to others.

The conformity of adultist children shows that they aren't really adults. They save themselves from despair by being rational, serious, and prematurely responsible, but they have not found fulfillment. The problem, in fact, is one of parenthood: such children are not in their right place in the family. During their time of adultism they submit to weak people. But, since they are eager for the support of friends to help them achieve resilience, they manage to get free of this excessive devotion and resume a kind of development. Adolescence is a critical period in this process. In the search for a friend who is more robust than they are, "they behave like the children they never were."[85] What we see then is a strange patchwork of parental behaviors and childish demands. But in both cases they are leading someone else's life.

Micheline and her sister had had a wretched childhood in Martinique. After their father died of a mysterious illness, the mother and the two girls managed to return to France. The mother was distraught, and so the children took complete responsibility for her, constantly reassuring her but still doing well as nursing students.

Micheline met an optician whose strength and conviction of certainty made her feel safe. But when she married this man, she didn't realize the extent to which she was also marrying his family. When her mother-in-law fell ill, Micheline tended her with abnormal devotion. To cheer her up, she even handed over the baby she had just given birth to, though this gift/abandonment was very painful for her. Completely infantile when with her husband, she acted as a parent to her mother-in-law to the point of exhaustion, taking care of two households along with her rather demanding career.

One day the inevitable occurred: she fell into a depression from overwork. People who are excessively devoted always divest themselves of their possessions in order to give them to others. This makes them happy, but sometimes they break down. When Micheline had to take care of herself during her depression, she was ashamed of feeling better while her mother-in-law was still suffering. Barely well again, she returned to her relational strategy of overdevotion. Only after her third relapse did her husband, exasperated by so much goodness, intervene to make his wife take care of herself. So, like a good little girl, she obeyed and dared to become happy.

For this woman, resilience came by way of the depression that, with the help of a healthy husband, forced her to change. This is not an unusual path. Many people have begun to blossom out after a period of despondency marking the end of a costly lifestyle and a defense mechanism that did not respect the personhood of the injured party.

Part II

Unripe Fruit, or the Age of Sex

30. Narration Is Not the Return of the Past

The healthiest and least costly path is that of storytelling. We must be competent tellers of our own story if we are to have an image of our own personality.

This task is oddly pleasant. It's easy to understand the delight we take in recalling happy memories. Bonds of affection form, and past happiness returns, when we share the joys of reminiscence in a group. But when we keep dwelling on a painful episode, bring back sad images, rehash conflictual conversations and imagine similar ones, we have a disconcerting sense of happy grief. This strangeness probably explains the function of internal narration: we once more take hold of the emotion aroused by the past and rework it into an inner self-image we can live with.

This process has a twofold effect. The first one has to do with identity: "I'm the person who escaped from juvenile detention and sent my father to prison in order to protect my sisters." The second involves the reworking of emotions: "I can now deal with the memory of the Chilean Army hunting down my mother and her children. Even twenty-five years later, I even feel somehow proud when I bring back this painful memory, since Spain, my host country, has given me important responsibilities."

Storytelling enables us to form an internal sense of ourselves, to take our place in the human world and share in its history. What is internally acceptable joins with what can be shared with others. Having done this work, the wounded person can look himself in the eye and rejoin society.

And so this is not the same as a return of the past, which is impossible. When I relate my visit to the palace of King Michael in Rumania, I don't bring back the memory of the four-hour trip to Constanza. I barely remember the thickness of the forest, the sultriness of the weather, and the length of the trip. What I do is condense several images that were significant for me: the isolation of the castle and the bizarre changes of style from one room to the next, and I give these pictures a meaning that allows me to instantly evoke that trip to Rumania.

As for the truth of memories: they are true in the sense that chimeras are. Everything is true in this mythological monster with the chest of a lion, the belly of a goat, and the wings of an eagle. And yet there is no such beast in reality. It exists only as an image that the speaker shares with other members of his culture.

The result of this twofold effect is that personal or cultural narratives can construct a secure attachment figure in our mental world when early bonds were fragile. Whereas early attachment is imprinted in the child's temperament unbeknownst to his parents, a story can be worked on intentionally in psychotherapy, artistic creativity, or sociocultural debate. All of us have to go through this process so as to construct our identity and take up a position in the group. Those who are psychologically injured must do so with trauma in their memory and the eyes of society on the account they give of it, which does not necessarily mean making an inner wound public.

31. Every Account Is a Tool for Reconstructing One's World

Some people who have been badly hurt or unsupported by their environment give up and remain dazed, confused, and helpless with regard to the past as they chew over the damage that is still alive in their minds. Others, however, manage "the creation of an inner story necessary for psychological survival."[86]

The story presents real facts whose meaning depends on whoever is talking about them. The writer Georges Perec never saw the people around him disappearing, until one day he did. During World War II the disappearance of the Jews was seldom seen, but it was suddenly realized that they had indeed vanished. Georges recalled his father wearing the uniform of the French Foreign Legion. And then, one day . . . he wasn't there anymore. He remembered his mother taking him to the train station, and then . . . she wasn't there anymore. His world emptied out without apparent trauma. The rent was huge but invisible, and the child didn't understand any of it because we can't observe something that isn't there.

During his four-year psychoanalysis, he broke through the shell of his rationalizing defenses, recovering memories that, for him, became events that could mend the great rip in his life: "I would have liked to help my mother clear the kitchen table."[87] You can well imagine that loving such a memory means not having had a mother. An event is not what we can see or know about the past but what we make of it in our need to become someone. The blandest commonplace can contain the seed of a major internal event if it offers the wounded person a foothold and a procedure for seeking lost memories. An event is what we make of what happens to us, be it despair or glory.

In fact, the emotion associated with the event arises in retrospect, in the confluence of several interpersonal worlds. What the wounded person thinks about what happened, and what he feels, depends on the story he tells himself about it as much as on the one he tells others, to which must be added the story these others tell about it.

The act of storytelling can shape the emotion very differently, in accordance with the listener and the cultural context. The wounded person may hear: "You're exaggerating," "There's no evidence for what you're saying," "Poor guy—after what happened to you you're messed up for life," "Poor child, don't be afraid; I'm here," "Tell me all the horrid details; I love that stuff," "You were looking for trouble," or "I admire you for pulling through." Think up a response, any response, and be assured that it has been given.

This does not prevent the narrative structure of the wounded person's story from revealing what he feels, but the emotion of his inner life comes from totally different sources: his own sensitivities imprinted in his memory by the way those close to him expressed their feelings, the importance he attaches to the event, and the meaning that comes from his cultural context.

Antoine was stunned when the butcher gave him his father's watch. Yet it was a beautiful pocket watch, with its little chain and engraved case. But the boy who wanted to free himself from his foster family had become very anxious when the good butcher hoped to teach him his trade. The gift meant that the foster father wanted the child to continue in the same path, continuing to work alongside him and support him in his old age. In such a context, the gift of the watch meant taking his place in the generations of the family line. As we have seen, this is exactly what Antoine was afraid of, and so a pretty watch became a source of anxiety. Antoine's behavior changed after the gift event; he froze over and kept his distance.

So why make stories? Imagine that you're on vacation. It is September 11, 2001, and there has been an incredible attack in the United States. It's the only thing people are talking and thinking about. You're at the beach, waiting in line at the ice cream stand. Suddenly an accomplice in an experiment appears and for the next two minutes makes an incoherent speech, in which, by arrangement, he utters the words "flag," "blue water," and "divine music." He then runs away.

Could you possibly say nothing, express no emotion? The surprise has created the feeling of an event in you. You smile, you act astonished, and you try out some sort of interpretation. But when your accounts of what happened are gathered together, a regularity slowly appears, for your interpretation of this unusual event reflects your cultural context.[88]

When we're at the beach, we expect "beach behavior" from others: stretching out on the sand, playing ball, or lining up for ice cream. If something unusual occurs, a small rip is made in your expectation. So why should you say, "He mentioned a 'flag,' which means he sees attacks everywhere," when other witnesses say, "I heard 'blue water'; he thinks this is bacteriological warfare," and others disagree: "Not at all; he's so stressed out these days that he's having a mystical hallucination of 'divine music.'"

You correctly perceived that something unusual was going on, something abnormal in the beach context, but in order to calm your little mental jolt you needed to give meaning to this inconsistency. So you integrated the event into a cultural context that is particularly disturbing to you as an individual, as it were digesting the events. Without this integration into a coherent account adapted to your context, you would feel at a loss, speechless, unable to see clearly, muster a response to the chaos, and restore a sense of inner peace.

If the words "flag," "blue water," and "divine music" have no meaning, the observer will be disoriented. If, on the other hand, the cultural context allows these incongruities to be interpreted, given a meaning, the observer will get his bearings once again. Every perception of an event calls for an initial act of psychological absorption. As soon as we can assign a meaning, we feel better because our world is now clear and we know what we have to do in it. In the flash of perception what we see and hear is already imbued with our subjectivity, our personal history, and our cultural context.

Accounts "can be 'real' or 'imaginary' without losing any of their force as stories."[89] What matters is that the story provides a reason. "He yelled 'flag' because of the attack, warning us that he saw something." Every story is a tool with which to construct our world. If we feel better as soon as we find ourselves thinking up a story, this is because the orientation, the meaning assigned to what we perceive takes us out of the realm of the absurd and supplies a reason.

32. To Struggle and Then to Dream

While, as we have seen, we all have to tell stories, some stories are harder to invent. The things we might want to say are not all equivalent: "My dad bought a bike" isn't the same as "My dad was shot before my eyes." Thinking back to a sweet pleasure, you might say, "I learned about sexual feelings when I kissed a cousin on the cheek, very close to her lips." But how to admit: "I learned about sexual pleasure at the age of 11, when my father came into my bed. I felt shame, pleasure, anxiety, and fear"?[90] A child can be driven from his culture by what you let escape you when you hear something like this: a horrified expression, a fixed smile.

When you live in distress, any kind of headlong flight provides a mad hope. How could it be otherwise? Daydreams let us fill our inner world with the feelings aroused by the story we invent. We feel better, the past gets lighter, reality becomes gentler. But such a daydream is a means of protection, a delicate balance. For there to be resilience, daydreams must coexist with the ideal self.

This is a private moment when we stage a playlet in our inner theater as a sample of our desires: "He'd do x, and I'd say y to him." What the dreamer "projects ahead of him as an ideal self is a substitute for the lost self-centeredness of his childhood."[91] When an infant feels an emotion, he expresses it with all his being, without negotiating with his environment. Only when he has come to understand the constraints of reality and the need to take the world of others into account does he give up his omnipotence. But in order to bear this limitation he invents an inner world in which he continues to fulfill his wishes. It is then that he experiences the feelings aroused by dreams. When a teenager dreams that he will win the Nobel Prize someday, that the whole world will be grateful to him, and that he will remain wonderfully unaffected despite his immense success, he regales himself with the self-image he is inventing.

The resilient attitude consists in asking oneself, "What am I going to do with my wound? Am I going to seek refuge in daydreams from time to time, finding nuggets of beauty there that will enable me to endure reality and sometimes even make it more beautiful?" A non-resilient mode of defense would say, "I'm going to live in a world of images and words cut off from this unbearable reality. What's happening inside me? How can I be inventing stories of a marvelous self when I have to acknowledge that my reality is pathetic?"

The two aspects of the ideal self are close to one another. A simple encounter, an expression, or an event can orient the wounded person toward either creative resilience or mythomania that combines imaginary glory and humiliation by reality. In this sense, creativity is a bridge of resilience between the calming daydream and the construction of an imaginary life. Mythomania, on the other hand, by merely masking shame, represents a failure of resilience.

When reality drives us to despair, daydreaming is a protective factor. I have had occasion to meet a Polish writer who had been deported to Auschwitz because of a trivial conflict with a German officer. Stupefied by reality, numbed by what he saw, he rushed to the safe haven of Proust's writings, trying to recall them the way someone struggles not to drown. In this context, daydreaming offered protection insofar as it replaced an unbearable reality. Since remembering a single sentence would take him a quarter of an hour, thanks to Proust he managed to create little islands of beauty for himself amid all the terror. If, after being freed, he had continued to take refuge in his daydream, he would have cut himself off from interpersonal relationships and become desocialized. So he found a bridge of resilience between daydreaming and his social context: he became a translator of Proust.

Depending on context, then, this defense mechanism may be constructive or destructive. It is even a rule that everyone in a difficult situation will react by struggling and then, immediately afterwards, by dreaming, testing out imaginary scenarios. When we are attacked, we are startled at first, and then we try to understand in order to find a solution. Taking action and daydreaming are the two defenses used in an emergency. Altruism, sublimation, anticipation, and humor—which are other resilience factors—call for some distance in time.

Our masters in dreaming are the artists who stage our internal debates, making pictures out of our social conflicts and stories out of our ordeals. They transform our unspeakable sufferings into poetry. An author who described an obscene reality without transforming it would be indecent, an additional aggressor. But one who can transfigure the unbearable, giving it an understandable and communicable form, helps us master the horror.

Anna Freud spoke of fantasies that reverse the actual situation.[92] At the moment of the traumatic rift we struggle through as best we can, but then daydreaming provides a pictorial form for the return of hope. As soon as he finds someone to tell about what happened, the wounded person begins to regain control of his history. This is slow work, however, since the mending process requires a host of encounters. The victim must learn to tell his story in an acceptable manner. Since it is indecent to describe things as they are, style becomes his tool for communication. Elegance, mannerism, allusion, derision, emphasis, humor, and the like make this task possible. In life "some things are so hard to bear that we can only speak lightly of them."[93] Theater, painting, and theorization take part in this work of alleviation. When the distant gaze of intellectualization keeps emotion at bay, the wounded person regains a bit of self-mastery.

This is why writing so often makes it possible to mend a torn self. Thanks to writing, I can slightly open the crypt containing unspeakable things, give voice to the locked-up ghosts who appear in my nightmares. Fifty percent of women writers and 40 percent of their male counterparts have suffered major traumas in childhood. This is a much higher figure than for the general population, and considerably more than the 5 percent who turn to politics and schools of higher learning.[94]

33. The Make-Believe Menagerie and the Family Novel

Children who don't know how to write or don't have a sense of time
sufficient to construct a narrative tell themselves two kinds of fables
every night: the serial adventures of the imaginary companion and the
family novel.

The make-believe menagerie plays a large role in a child's psychological development. Before going to bed, every child knows that in order to
nod off, he must leave reality and slip into another world, the world of
sleep. He has to have had a good day and be trusting enough to let go of
his hold on reality, letting himself glide toward a shadow world in which
all the ghosts can come forth. So he invents an intermediate stage in which
he imagines beings that are strange and yet familiar, not entirely unknown.

Every evening he replays the scene of the little boy who invites into
his bed Pernou, his nice invisible friend who is half human and half dog,
and Perguit, another animal/human friend. Reassured by the fine company he has invented for himself, he dares to take the plunge into night.
The imaginary animals populate this intermediate zone between the
familiar parent who keeps him safe and the scary unknown. It makes no
difference to the child that he himself is the author of this realm, since
the evocation of this realm makes him feels better. His imagination acts
on his inner reality as the two "buddies" alter his inner world, calm his
anxiety, and invite him to let himself drift off to sleep in good company.
There is no creation without an effect. Everything that is invented acts
on the inventor's psyche.

From his first writings on, Freud stressed the importance of the family romance (that is, the family novel), when the child makes up a story
or says that his family isn't his real family.[95] "It's an accident of life that
placed me with these people," a little girl might say. "I know I'm a princess, since I look so much like Queen Fabiola. Besides, one day I saw
the people who pretend to be my parents talking with a funny-looking
bum. They were surely giving him the money they'd promised him for
kidnapping me."

The child who tells herself this fable and elaborates it each time she

discovers a new sign is working deep within herself to develop her budding sense of autonomy: "I'm learning that my parents aren't the exceptional beings I thought they were. I want to identify with people who
are more like me, such as a queen. The scary incestuous desire I've felt
isn't guilty, since the men in my family aren't my real father and brother.
So what I felt is normal."

Don't think that this family novel indicates contempt for the true parents. It's almost the opposite. As he grows up, the child discovers his parents' limitations. He is nostalgic for his past admiration, but thanks to the
family novel, he avoids disappointment and inwardly cherishes the delightful feelings from the time when his parents were still prestigious. This
is how an imaginary creation reworks a real feeling from the past. Later,
when the older child or adolescent meets a friend with a similar imagination, they will create a joint daydream validating their shared feelings.
Faith is at work, altering reality and drawing the faithful toward delight
. . . or horror.

"Whereas sublimation takes other people's existence into account, daydreaming is an expression of narcissism."[96] If the environment is empty,
the person is a prisoner of his refuge and runs the risk of staying locked
up there, as is the case with mythomania. But if he manages to find someone who invites him to make the effort to transform his daydream into an
act of creativity, the wounded person can build a bridge of resilience.

A traumatized child who does not dream remains subject to a destructive reality. In contrast, a shattered child who takes refuge in dreams to
the point of cutting himself off from reality is desocializing himself. Only
the injured child who protects himself through daydreaming and meets
someone who encourages a creative effort will have opportunities to become resilient.

Fleeing reality or submitting to it are two toxic defense mechanisms,
but protecting oneself from an assaultive reality and finding in the imagination some reasons to change it is a resilient defense. "From the wounds
of childhood and the heaviness of buried memories artists draw new
strength as they reinvent their history. Close to dreaming, . . . this self-
transformation tends to enlarge our restricted notion of the individual."[97]

34. Giving Form to the Shadow in Order to Reconstruct Oneself: The Omnipotence of Despair

I like to say that what can't be expressed directly can always be expressed sideways. This is a way of referring to the challenge of transformation when handicaps, suffering, or shame change into personal flourishing as soon as they are confronted. Every well-brought-up hero has to surmount an ordeal as part of his journey toward the light. But a traumatized person can only choose between annihilation and fighting: "I really felt I was going under. For life to lose all meaning like this, there's no suffering like it. . . . All I was at that time was an overflowing activity, and I discovered the omnipotence of despair."[98] When we are hurtling toward death, the urgent defense is to struggle, even if we are sometimes tempted to slip into the abyss. If we stand up to the absurdity of life before nothingness forces itself on us, we will be able to fill the void and become creators.[99]

The normal person's path has its tribulations: he bumps up against stones, gets scratched on brambles, hesitates at the dangerous places, and, in the end, makes his way nonetheless. But the traumatized person's path is broken. There is a hole, a collapse that leads to the precipice. When he stops and turns back, he makes himself a prisoner of his past, a fundamentalist, or an avenger, or he submits to the precipice that is so close to him, whereas the resilient person, when he stops, continues along a lateral course. He has to clear a new path, keeping in mind the edge of the ravine. The normal walker may become creative; the resilient person is forced to.

When the perceived reality can't be integrated, the child feels that a bomb is going off inside him: "Why here, or there, or anywhere else? Why this instead of some other thing?" His shattered identity can no longer handle the information coming in from the world and adjust to it. It is urgent that he give form to this uproar and get a grip on himself again. By bringing coherence to his perceived world, the child becomes capable of an adaptive response: fleeing; submitting; or seducing, confronting, or analyzing the aggressor in order to control him.

The most common emergency defense mechanism is the symptom, an observable phenomenon expressing a part of the invisible inner world. As soon as the symptom illustrates the pulverization of the internal world, the person can pinpoint an image for his own unhappiness and hence feels better. He knows where the pain comes from and can finally give a name to it. This body schema gives a shape to his disarray and allows him to communicate the suffering: "I can join a group and express what I'm feeling. I can consult a doctor and show him a symptom. I'm no longer alone in the world. I now know what I have to deal with and how to get help from people close to me and from my culture."

"This figuration is an avatar of anxiety, a descent into the outline of the image, . . . a transformation of an inassimilable reality [into a form] that changes the nature of the trauma and regulates it."[100]

When a trauma tears the personality apart, pulverizes it, or shatters it more or less seriously, the wounded person is confused for awhile, without a sense of identity: "What's happening to me? What should I do in this case?" If his troubled memory retains a sense of the person he used to be and the family surrounding him, he takes the shadow of his past with him, a strange witness, an impalpable proof that he was someone. And so, deep inside his shattered self, there is still a wavering affirmation, a presence of another place, an ember of life:

> When I get back on track, when I return to the light of day to find a little happiness, I see the shadow I'm projecting: it's the shadow of my dead parents. I'm a real image, I'm a boy, I'm not good at soccer, and I have a lot of friends, but other people can easily see that I have two shadows in me, and so they mistrust me and find me skittish:
>
> "What's wrong with that boy? He's good-looking and nice, but suddenly his language has holes in it. He falls silent when we talk about our parents and freezes up when we run and hug them. What's wrong with that boy? He charms us but makes us uneasy. Even when he's there with us, he seems to be off in the distance and brings back a relic, an old-fashioned photo

with zigzag edges. He looks at it often; it's the photo of his
shadows. Sometimes an object comes to him from the beyond,
a cardboard box with the corners caved in, a coin from a foreign country, a little gold key he surely inherited from his
paternal shadow."[101]

The name I bear is that of my shadows, the social evidence that they
really existed. My ghosts were real. My history grows heavy with the
history of my shadows. What do you do to feel the weight of a shadow?
Do you go to ground in the shadow so as not to have a shadow anymore? Do you melt into the crowd, seek anonymity, so as to become a
nobody of a person? But when you want to live despite the burden of
the shadows, you change your name, and, in order to hide it better, put
it up in lights:

> I'll call myself Niki de Saint-Phalle. This cryptonym will
> travel across the world and take its place among the human-
> ity from which I was expelled at the age of 11, when my fa-
> ther, that great banker I loved so much, came into my bed. I'll
> fight against my exile, I'll sculpt images of gals with bullseyes
> on their genitals, I'll give flesh to my shadow and matter to
> my trauma. Then those creatures who were evicted from my
> private world will make my name acceptable. I'll rejoin the
> world of human beings with the wound I'll have made into
> works of art.[102]

Putting outside oneself the traumatic crypt forming a cyst in the psyche
is one of the most effective resilience factors. To this end, the mutilated
child must have become able to find a cultural setting and a mode of expression appropriate for him.[103]

Writing offers this means of resilience very early on, a way to exter-
nalize, make visible and malleable, a pain deep inside the self. It is a
mystery how many traumatized children want to become writers when
they still don't know how to write. Writing isn't speaking. When I tell

about my wound, other people's facial expressions, exclamations, or even silences have an effect on my emotions. Merely their mute presence makes them the co-authors of what I say. I'm no longer the sole master of my wishes. It's hard for me to get a grip on my feelings about the past. The listener has influenced my intentions.

In contrast, when I write with the words I'm looking for in the rhythm that suits me, I put outside me, set down on paper, the crypt from which, each night, ghosts would come forth.

Just as Niki de Saint-Phalle rejoins the human world by fashioning "gals" whose genitals are targets, Francis Ponge places outside himself a piece of writing whose private function is to repair him: "It's as though, since I began writing, I were running 'after' the respect of a certain person."[104] Writing is a plea. Every novel puts a redeeming hero onstage. The work extends the psychic apparatus and gives a sculptural or written form to the shadow the wounded person carries within him: "This place is an external forum containing a delegation of representatives from the internal forum."[105] The place of the work is the place of the crypt, the theater in which ghosts enact their dramas. Proust, an expert in evoking shadows, knew well that what he was writing about was his past life.[106]

35. Books About the Self Alter Reality

Erich von Stroheim, the author of his own story, spent his life transforming his painful past. If he had written a realistic account of it, he
would have said that he was born in Vienna of pious Jewish parents who
sold hats,[107] and everyone would have died of boredom. He would have
related how, at the end of his life, after finding renown in America, he
was ruined and brought down by a series of catastrophes. His daughter, whose face had been severely burned, could not leave the hospital,
his son was risking death, and he had to sell everything he owned in
order to pay for his wife's upkeep. His friends found him a job as an
editor of film scripts, and Erich "invented" disfigured heroines treated
by poor but worthy doctors, famous psychiatrists brought low by ad-
versity who resembled . . . you guessed it.

Daydreaming is a defense that offers protection from the horror, the
coldness and pain, of reality by creating a warm private world. When
fiction manages to act on facts, reality becomes poeticized, but if there
is too great a break with reality, daydreaming can become a logical delusion or a form of mythomania.

At the age of 10, Charles Dickens worked twelve hours a day in a
shoe-polish factory in which human relationships were desperate. He
was then sent to school at Wellington House Academy, where it was
felt to be a moral obligation to beat the boys every day as part of their
training. From the time he was 15, Dickens held public readings in
which he acted out the tribulations of his life that he was beginning to
write down.[108]

One day, when he was finding his life very hard, he passed by the castle
at Gad's Hill Place and began to dream that he lived there, and that the
mere fact of living amid such beauty made him happy. Several years later,
when he was extremely successful and rich, he bought this castle and was
not always happy there. Yet the dream had protected him, even enchanted
him, enabling him to build an inner world full of hope and beauty.

Literature about inner life has been long in coming. At first, the "I"
was a notarized act ("I own three goats, am selling two, sign my name").

Then it became an internalized account believed to be private even though it was still social ("I met the king," "I set out for the war"). The modern "I" that dares to relate its journeys in the inner world is very recent, even though an occasional great figure like St. Augustine or Jean-Jacques Rousseau was able to escape social constraints to attempt this personal adventure. "The explosion of personal literature beginning at the end of the eighteenth century bears witness to a new social concept of personal privacy."[109]

Conversely, one of the first signs of totalitarianism is the burning of books in order to hinder the expression of different mental worlds. Dictatorship involves governing souls, to the point where the politics of confession becomes the way to control private realms. The existence of a literature of inner lives could thus reveal the degree to which a society is democratic.

From the onset of its popularity in the eighteenth century such writing has had a therapeutic effect: a glazier "writes every day to bring back the memory of his wife, who died five years earlier."[110] He was thus able to keep on living with her a little longer and to hold onto some beautiful moments from the past. Writing about one's wound also changes the way the person affirms himself. The spoken past creates an intersubjectivity, whereas the written past is addressed to the ideal reader, the invisible friend, the other self. This means that the written world is in no way the translation of the spoken world; it is the invention of an additional awareness, the acquisition of strength to stand firm in the presence of others.

When childhood cares became a social preoccupation, the fairy tales of Charles Perrault or the Brothers Grimm described the social condition of the children to whom they were addressed. "Tom Thumb" spoke of abandonment and "Donkey Skin" of incest at a time when children were often just extra mouths to feed and incestuous fathers were not only not sent to prison but were even invited to their daughter's wedding.[111]

36. The Literature of Resilience Works Far More Toward Freedom Than Toward Revolution

In the nineteenth century there appeared a fine literature of resilience in which little children are taken away from their tender home. Hector Malot describes the unbelievable condition of workers whose relatives would starve to death when an accident caused the wage-earner his job.[112] *Les Misérables* gives life to Cosette, who speaks for thousands of abandoned and exploited little girls. *Oliver Twist* and *David Copperfield* are a kind of autobiography written in the third person, in which the little hero represents the author.

All these accounts of resilience have the same narrative structure. They tell the edifying story of a fine child who has lost his family because of the cruelty of wicked people. Nevertheless, thanks to providence, they eventually find happiness through encounters with good people. The moral of the story is that children seem bad because they were mistreated. But make no mistake: they were born into good families, right-thinking and industrious. These children may have appeared to be dirty, unhappy thieves, but, being of good quality, all they have to do is find a kind, middle-class substitute family and everything will turn out well in the end.

In the nineteenth century the wounded child becomes a subject for literature because he provides an example of virtue: "And so readers will be interested in this little book in which three children from different countries, from very poor families, tell in their own voices how, after much suffering, they moved up in the world by dint of hard work, merit, and honesty, achieving good positions and whatever happiness, comfort, and respect one could ask for in this world."[113]

In the twentieth century the findings of psychoanalysis did not ignore social causes. When a man is driven away because of incest, deportation, or poverty, he has to follow the same path of resilience as an immigrant or an exile. Exclusion is the characteristic course in our societies: 15 percent of the population of the West today is excluded, as opposed to 50 percent of Africans and 70 percent of South Americans. Is it possible to become a human being outside of the realm of humanity? If the organization of their community so allows, they can regain a place in society only by searching for the meaning of their upheaval and reconstructing their identity all over again.[114]

Autobiography or the account given of one's life is not the return of the real past but a representation of this real past that makes it possible for us to reidentify ourselves and seek an appropriate social position.[115] But since the individual has become a primary value in the modern West, this inner work, this quest for private meaning to bring about self-realization, is proof of democracy.

This inner process is countered in totalitarian societies, where, as Solzhenitsyn has written, people aren't even sure they have the right to relate the events of their private lives.[116] In a democracy, on the other hand, we are invited "to seek and construct meaning based on personalized temporal facts."[117]

The oscillation between private and public life is illustrated by the disappearance of autobiographies in France between 1940 and 1970. The collapse brought on by the war and the need for reconstruction had given so much priority to social discourses that any personal expression seemed indecent: victims were silenced in favor of myths. A violent dad was unthinkable in a culture where fathers were glorified. A child of collaborators had no right to complain when the official account heaped scorn on his parents. As for incestuous fathers and mothers, it would have been obscene to mention them at a time when what one had to do was dream of the reconstruction of an idyllic family life.

After 1970, the explosion of the literature of the self bears witness to a cultural change. We are at peace, society is affluent, the adventure of the individual is exalted. People are thrilled to read about the daily life of a peasant in Brittany or a village in Provence, of someone who explored the Arctic or strange destinies.

The readers of these personal accounts are looking for a mirror so as not to be alone anymore in their own private lives. Thus we find authors of a single book: the movie star who writes with the help of a ghost-writer, the statesman who has no time to read his own book, the celebrity who becomes the emblem of a social group, and the thousands of little people who write the thousands of inexpensive little books found in bins outside bookstores today.

37. Making Believe In Order to Fabricate a World

Writing is the alchemy that transforms our past into a work of art, plays a role in the reconstruction of a damaged self, and enables us to be acknowledged by our society. But before writing, other socially validated modes of self-representation are established in the course of development.

From the age of 15 months on, a child has to know how to "make believe." He has to fall although he is not being forced to, and he has to simulate tears and pain that he isn't actually feeling. He has to know how to seem to be threatening, asleep, or even affectionate. In short, all the basic activities of his life must be staged in his little preverbal theater if he is to have access to otherness. The moment a child begins to invent a character and brings it to life—an imaginary double to whom he confides his little disappointments, a preverbal role he enacts with gestures, facial expressions, postures, and vocalizations—he shows adults that he understands the existence of a mental world other than his own and that he is trying to influence it with his imaginary scenarios.

Make-believe is an intellectual feat, since it allows not only for the child's expression of his private world but also for intersubjective mastery: "I'm going to get her stirred up by making myself fall. I'll get her to rescue and protect me by pretending to cry." Fifteen months later, when the child begins to master speech, he will use words to accomplish the same thing. In telling a story, he will express his inner world and manipulate your emotions, thereby forming the bond he needs. But in order for this creation of a virtual world to be effective, the other person—the adult or friend—must respond authentically to the make-believe because he is not playing; what he feels is "for real."

When the child is alone in an empty world, when reality is terrifying and he protects himself by inventing a fiction, if the other person does not respond to this virtual world the child remains imprisoned in what he had just invented. Lying can be a useful defense, but mythomania is a perverted attempt at resilience because those around the wounded child didn't respond so as to give the defense a socially communicable form.

When reality is bearable because it is not disturbing, because you have your place in it and have established relationships, it is friendly, interesting, and even more fun than games of fiction, and the child learns to make his way in his milieu. But when reality is frightening, when social or affective relationships are dangerous or humiliating, fabrication enables the child to protect himself from the outer world by surrendering to the world he invents.

38. Lying Is a Bulwark Against Reality; Mythomania Conceals Shabbiness

Lying protects the child when he is in danger; mythomania restores his feeling of self-worth when there is no way to mend his impaired image. In the latter case, the stories he makes up about himself become too coherent to be honest.

Reality is always a bit chaotic: we make mistakes about dates, have ambivalent feelings, and find inconsistencies in our images of the past. But someone who fabricates stories must be coherent to the point of absurdity, drawing bits of truth from the narratives around him and creating a fiction out of them. Whereas a child with a serene attachment plays at fiction when he practices taking his place in his environment, a little mythomaniac takes refuge in fiction to avoid that world or convey a favorable image with which he can enter his society. He is afraid of the real world, yet he wants to find a place in it. So he slips in by creating the image those around him expect.

This is why the themes of mythomania are those of our own lives: social success, physical adventures, military exploits, or even charming little daily triumphs: "She was so pretty, and we went for a walk," says the teenager who is miserable because he doesn't dare to smile at a girl. As he is relating his fable, he feels the emotion aroused by the image of himself that he is presenting.

Emotional deprivation is at the heart of these compensatory fictions. It is the primary cause of mythomania, which can exacerbate it in turn. It is a failed defense. Daydreaming, on the other hand, is a metaphor for our desires, since it portrays what we aspire to and trains us to make the wish a reality. But in mythomania we talk a lot of hot air in order to fill the affective void for the moment. This is not a good situation. We may soar smoothly through the little playlet while we're staging it, but then we have to come back down to earth, and, as with all drugs, we have to move on quickly to the next high.

A child in a context of emotional isolation almost always ends up drifting into first psychological and then physical death. But occasionally, even in cases of extreme privation, we see one who resists: a child who manages to create an inner world constructed from a few clues, a few negligible bits and pieces. After extracting two or three perceptions from the surrounding reality, the child turns them into an object of hyperattachment.[118] He overinvests a photo, a piece of gift wrap, a gilded nail, a ribbon, or a newspaper article that becomes a treasure he hides under his pillow. This object symbolizes an attachment that has been lost and then regained: "My father would have given me this," "It's the sort of present a mother would give her child." This object that an adult would see as worthless and meaningless is a precious pearl for its little owner, material proof of the possibility of loving. A scrap of paper can become the bearer of hope. And yet the child knows quite well that he has invented this object and invested it with the emotional power he needs so much.

When the older child or adolescent fabricates a story, he is doing the same thing. He invents a little play showing his desires, and, as he is enacting it with words and gestures, he experiences what he had just invented.

As we have seen, the purpose of the three virtual worlds of lying, mythomania, and daydreaming is to provide a sense of security. Lying protects like a rampart, mythomania like a seductive image, and daydreaming like a drawbridge to the countryside. But when there is no countryside the drawbridge leads nowhere, and the child remains the prisoner of his invention. In other words, it is a relationship with another person, with the family and society, that transforms daydreaming into creativity or, instead, into a mirage. Mythomania is a failed attempt at resilience because the injured child hasn't encountered an environment that can accept him with his wound.

I am fond of the proverb, undoubtedly Chinese, that says, "The facade of the house belongs to whoever is looking at it." The person who lives in the house builds a facade as a gift to the spectator. But when we know the benefits a gift provides to the giver, we can understand that the distraught child who builds himself a fabulous facade is actually trying to make an emotional bridge between himself and those around him.

Yet all he can offer is a pretty facade of himself, because his reality is too sad. Behind the stage set is ruination and despair. He will at least have existed as a pretty picture in your mind, shared with you a lovely dream, but this is all the benefit he gets from the gift of a facade that masks rubble.

If you break through his stage set you injure him twice. First, you send him back to his sordid reality, and then you humiliate him by discovering his deception. So he'll run away to hide from reality and save the facade, his imaginary dignity. If you make his reality bearable, he will have less need for his mythomania. His daydreams will once again become samplings of pleasure and metaphors for projects. From then on, fantasy, not deception, will be what protects him. He can use it to make a story or go onstage without swindling the spectator. Everything is clear: this is just a story, a picture, a legend, a theatrical piece. But deep inside, the wounded child has regained mastery over his unhappiness, which you bandage by applauding him. The distance in time, the search for words, and the skillfulness of the presentation enable him to get free of his trauma and even make it into a bridge to society.

Jorge Semprun illustrates this process very well, starting with the injury and gradually moving toward fiction as he puts his trauma into a communicable form.[119] Thirty years after being deported, he manages to bear witness by mingling facts and imagination. Picasso recognized that he was following the same path when he painted *Guernica*, an almost colorless allegory, to signify death. For forty years Steven Spielberg made use of denial to protect himself from the pain of the Holocaust. But in the end it was a fiction, the film *Schindler's List*, that made him whole again. Even his choice of subject was an autobiographical confession. In telling the story of a man who saved thousands of Jews during World War II, Spielberg gave form to his wish to believe that, in spite of everything, the world did contain a few generous men.

39. The Power of Fiction Lies Much More in Persuasion Than in Explanation

No fiction is invented from nothing. There are always some signs of reality nourishing the imagination. Even the most unrestrained daydreams give form to fantasies that come from our inner world, sometimes close to the unconscious.

When J. K. Rowling wrote the Harry Potter series,[120] she chose to call the hero's best friend Weasly, a name close to the sound of *measly*, which means "pitiful like a child with measles." In a single evocative sound, she populated Harry's world with pitiful kids. The author herself belonged to this kind of reality, but she protected herself by imagining that toads could teach you how to defend yourself against the forces of evil. At the age of 6 she wrote her first story, "Rabbit," to keep her little sister from being hurt by reality. And when, as an adult, she was once again attacked by reality, she found a way to defend herself by writing *Harry Potter*. Each time Rowling had to deal with another trauma, the writing of the series would take another turn. In short, she was writing a "false fiction," since the story was not false but allowed her to express the transformation of her pain into a magical tale for the delight of society.

This resilient passage from real pain to the pleasure of representing that pain blames society far more than it blames the injured person. Why does the public find it so hard to hear testimonies? Or rather, why can it hear only testimonies that confirm the way it sees itself? Fred Uhlman, the son of a German-Jewish doctor, wanted to bear witness to the disappearance of half of his classmates, Jews and non-Jews, in 1942. When he wrote, "I saw that twenty-six out of the forty-six of the boys in my class had died," he induced a numb silence. Bewildered, he hesitated a bit: "Did I really want or need to know?" But then, in order to speak the truth that no one wanted to hear, he decided to write his book,[121] in which, like Semprun, Picasso, Rowling, and many others, he invented a fiction that gave the truth a socially acceptable form. He describes his

teenage friendship with Count von Hohenfels, executed at the age of 16
for having plotted against Hitler while his parents, splendid aristocrats,
were involved in the destruction of the Jews in Europe.

Fiction has a much greater power of persuasion than personal testimony because the plot line wins allegiance better than mere attestation,
which is too close to the obscene pronouncements of the government:
"55 percent of the children died at an average age of 15 years, 3 months,"
or "90 percent were admitted to the advanced class in high school," and
the like.

Emotional denial facilitates revisionist ideas:

> Wednesday, June 14, 1916
>
> Dear Mother,
> I returned safely from my home leave and found my battalion
> without too much difficulty. . . . As you might expect, like all
> my buddies I found that these past two years of war had gradu-
> ally led to egoism and indifference in the civilian population
> and that we fighters had nearly been forgotten. . . . Some people
> almost gave me to understand that they were amazed I hadn't
> yet been killed. . . . So I'll try to forget, just as I have been
> forgotten.
>
> Good-bye. I'm sending you a million kisses with all my heart,
> Gaston[122]

When we keep silent, we die even more. But when we bear witness,
we encounter silence. Given such a painful choice, fiction becomes a good
way to make reality bearable. But a writer who invents a story based on
his memory serves up what we hope for: some fine stories about war, love,
solidarity, triumph over evil, pomp and glory, the revenge of the power-
less, magic, fairies, and tenderness. All the great moments in the life of
the listener are portrayed by a writer who tells his own story.

40. Prisoner of a Story

When Jean-Claude Romand is afraid to present himself for the second-year examination in medicine, he finds himself alone and utterly deserted.[123] He had never wanted to do anything other than be a doctor, and his failure drives him into a deep depression. Prisoner of a single dream, he has no alternative plan. It is impossible for him to admit how desolate and lifeless he feels.

But an imaginative leap can still keep him alive: he'll say that he passed, went on with his studies, and became a research physician with the World Health Organization. Then he'd see with his own eyes how impressed and happy he had made his parents. Romand feels renewed through his dazzling fiction. His representation has altered reality.

Outside this story he is nobody. His only sense of being alive comes through words, and giving up this illusion would plunge him into the void of non-existence: "What can you say, what can you relate, when you experience nothing, when you kill time reading all the newspapers in your car parked in a supermarket parking lot, when you doze off all alone in a cafe, when you spend your time in bed looking at the ceiling?"[124]

Reality is sickening for such a person, and there is no beauty except in the imagination. So he has to find some signs of truth to serve as a basis for a magnificent story, a verbal image of himself to be offered to those he loves. One evening Bernard Kouchner signs one of his books for Romand: "With best wishes." Now there is a sign of reality, a basis for demonstrating his friendship with the heroic doctor with whom he "worked at the WHO." On one occasion, Romand relates, he and his lover were invited to dinner with Kouchner at Fontainebleau. He takes his car, pretends to be lost as he consults his map, and acts as though he's looking for his friend's house: "There's the sign for the intersection at Tronces. It's not very far now."

This is a brief triumph, because reality always takes revenge. His lover is surprised by certain inconsistencies, but she brings about the return of reality mainly by asking when Jean-Claude will be able to repay the large sum of money she had loaned him.

The theater of beauty collapses; he comes up against the hideous reality and panics. He begins to strangle his mistress. But don't think this is an attempted murder; rather, it is a melancholy declaration of love: "There was not much difference between him and his love objects."[125] When death is welcome, when he wants to kill himself to get free of reality, the melancholic isn't quite sure whether he's murdering himself or the woman he loves. This is why, later, when reality can no longer be escaped, Jean-Claude Romand, in his "great kindness," shoots and kills his daughter, his son, his wife, his mother, his father, and even his dog to keep them from suffering the disillusionment of a descent into reality.

This terrifying defense might have turned out differently. The proof is that the process cured him. "Condemned to live" after his attempted suicide, Jean-Claude finally feels alive. The moment he has no choice and must accept the lawyers' visits, see the judge, and obey the rules about walks, tasks, mail, and meetings, he finds reality bearable. A chaplain helps him discover spirituality, which is another way to escape and resist reality, but this time by transcending it.[126] He speaks, writes, meditates, and learns Japanese, and women fall in love with this exceptional man: "I was never so free, and life was never so beautiful. . . . I am a murderer, [but] this is easier to bear than twenty years of falsehood."[127]

Freed by being imprisoned, he may have thought as follows: "I no longer need to lie. I was a prisoner of my imaginary defense, but I find that the reality of prison is more pleasant and more alive than the melancholy void I experienced before. Under these conditions I can become myself again. Now that confession has brought me back to the world, you will have to love me as I am, with my crimes and my past."

This need to encounter others, to test himself against reality, to get lumbered with facts and then give them meaning, was never suggested to Jean-Claude Romand. It's easy to be a good, transparent student: all you have to do is be afraid of life. Then you slow down, get into the routine of your desk in your room, do some reading here and there, repeat more or less what is expected, pass some exams, and your parents are proud of this dismal success. If you want to feel alive even so, you dream, picturing the life you aspire to. When no one invites you out of yourself, dreams end up cutting you off from reality, which has become more bland and sickening than ever. Your sole pleasure remains imaginary.

A bridge of resilience can't be constructed unless the dreamer awakes and the culture makes some possibilities available to him for work and especially for encounters with others. It was prison that offered this to Romand.

41. The Reparative Power of Fictions Can Alter Reality

Society can offer gentler places for healing than prison. This is what happened for Erich von Stroheim: "He used lying to protect his privacy but also to construct himself. He succeeded so well in this that his only remaining way to reach his true personality was the creation of masterpieces."[128]

Erich von Stroheim compensated for the shame of his youth with an excess of imagination. Born in Vienna in 1885, in 1906 he enlisted in the military unit known as "the dragoons of Moses" because many Jewish soldiers were in it. The following year he became a corporal but was soon declared unfit for service. In 1909 he got on a ship in Bremen, and by the time he arrived in New York ten days later he had added a "von" to his name. Like any poor immigrant, he worked at a thousand odd jobs until the day in 1914 when he was hired as an extra in Hollywood. We are far away from the fine cavalier, captain of the dragoons!

In the cultural context of the United States at that time, any man was invited to descend into reality and realize his wildest dreams. Humiliated by his discharge from the military, Erich took refuge in compensatory imaginings, but in American culture he was able to set in motion a process of resilience.

He first based his myth on actual details. Just as Romand read all the medical literature on cholesterol and walked up and down the WHO building in Geneva, Stroheim gathered plausible information that allowed him to describe the medal of the Order of Elisabeth supposedly conferred on his mother and the wound he supposedly received in Bosnia-Herzegovina.

Like all liars, he masked himself by playing the role of someone who can't tolerate lies. Having found a place where he could express his imagination, he could let "the image he gave in his films make real and true the person he wanted to be."[129] He was fond of relating how, when Goebbels, an expert on the army, saw *La Grande Illusion* in 1937 and exclaimed, "But we never had officers like that!" a spectator replied, "So much the worse for you!" (Stroheim disarmed critics with this anecdote.)

The transformation of the real little Jew into the aristocratic officer of his dreams made him a superstar. In a different sociocultural context his mythomania might have turned out badly. Like Romand's, perhaps.

This example also shows that there would be no mythomaniacs without those who adore myths, since the tales they serve up correspond to what we all hope for. Their fine stories flatter our most delusional wishes. The delightful complicity between the mythomaniac and his worshipers explains the large number of Louis XVIIs appearing in the Romantic period, the number of czarinas after the Russian Revolution of 1917, and the astounding number of physician-warriors and even Auschwitz survivors nowadays.[130]

Since the mythomaniac's fiction, with our agreement, assigns him a place in the dreams of a despairing society, he concludes that his imagination has altered reality and thus feels better. He had been enormously ashamed of the importance he attaches to the way he is viewed by others. But now everything has changed in the representation of reality and the resulting interactions. He has composed a portrait, a narrative identity that personalizes and comforts him so that, when he relates his fiction, he is dazzling in his simplicity and modesty. He must, of course, occasionally admit to himself that this identity is just a story, but he can't give up the advantages it brings. Fiction has great relational value because the story links the speaker to his audience. "The mythomaniac tells lies the way he breathes; if he didn't lie, he would stop breathing."[131] This is the only life he has.

The collective imagination, too, is organized this way. When a group is humiliated or desperate, it invents a beautiful tale of tragedy and glory to unite its members and repair their wounded self-esteem.

Jorge is a little Salvadorean boy of 8. His father emigrated to the United States, and his mother disappeared when he was 4. He was found wandering in the street, thin, numb, and filthy. A religious institution took him in, washing and feeding him in silence because the nuns were so overwhelmed with work. Jorge adapted to this wordless milieu. He continued developing slowly until the day when a group of soldiers tried to kidnap him as he left church in order to train him for war.[132]

The child fought back and succeeded in escaping. But from then on he began to dream aloud. At night, during his involuntary dreams, he would revisit the daydreams he had invented. He recounted the atrocities he supposedly witnessed and was surprised he didn't suffer because of them. When the adults wept and panicked, the child would appear serene. He couldn't know that dissociation between the memory of trauma and the numbness of the emotions is a classic symptom of psychological trauma.

Jorge thought he was stronger than the others, and this error protected him. He invented himself as a superman. He would relate how he could leap over mountains in a single bound and, with his great powers, guess what everyone was thinking and kill with one glance the wicked people who were trying to harm him. The nuns, having made the connection between the attempted kidnapping and this odd way of speaking, just sighed when they listened to him, but visitors were convinced that he was schizophrenic.

It was at this time that Jorge began to put his mythomania to the test in order to prove that he was telling the truth. He was doing better as a result of his incredible stories, regaining confidence, feeling safe, and, above all, establishing human relationships. He had occasional doubts, naturally, but at these moments of uncertainty when reality asserted itself he felt himself icing over and withdrawing from the world. So he had to prove that he was indeed a superman. He climbed the outer wall of a building bare-handed in order to feel the roughness, dived into a whirling torrent in order to let the water carry him away, and threw himself in front of cars in order to just miss getting hit by them. Each time he escaped death he felt more cheerful, having proved his invincibility. He felt better. People said he was crazy.

When we have lived through an extreme situation, when we have been banished from normality,[133] there are several possible strategies.

When the upheaval has been too great, we may find it oddly comforting to simply slip toward death. But when the injury hasn't totally destroyed us and the internal resources instilled in the course of our early attachments still give us the strength to cling to others, the reintegration into normality depends on our emotional, social, and cultural environment.

42. A 12-Year-Old War Veteran

There have always been child soldiers. Older boys who played the drums and fifes in the armies of the French Republic often fell on the front lines. The Marie-Louises of the Napoleonic armies and the older boys in the retreat of the Wehrmacht were sacrificed to delay the advance of the opposing army for a few hours. This is not counting the 14,000 little boys blown up during the Iran–Iraq War so that the adult soldiers could then attack on a battlefield free of land mines.

But the twentieth century invented a new way to be a child soldier. Boys are no longer just like soldiers, only smaller. Nowadays we prefer to make use of their characteristics as children in order to adapt them to modern guerrilla warfare. As the virtual war of machines is developing, actual battlefields are disappearing. Armies clash less and less in the open fields, more and more on street corners, village squares, and paths in the bush.[134] A handful of children armed with machine guns, pretty and light as toys, can easily block a road, control the passengers on a bus, and help in evicting people from their homes. These are wars without battlefronts in which unarmed civilians become targets so that families will be demoralized and those who have not entirely submitted to the aggressors' way of thinking will be disbanded. In this kind of war, children play a major role.

It feels odd to chat with a boy of 12 and have him tell you in all seriousness that he is a veteran of the war in Mozambique. He has just claimed his demobilization pay and is wondering what will become of him. Like two thousand of his little male friends and several girls he knew, he spent 5 years at war. He is an attractive little boy, but he looks strange, with an indefinable sense of uneasiness about him. He is too serious for his age.

Taken in by the Amosapu,[135] he is said to be very calm, distant, gloomy, and almost impervious to what is happening around him. He might be considered a hardboiled little character with no feelings were it not for the fact that, from time to time, he bursts out in rage or tears for some trivial cause. He acts like a little man and is annoyed when asked the kinds of questions usually addressed to children. If he did not appear so grown-up, so rational in his behavior, he would remind an observer of the icy vigilance of abused children.

He says he was not abused. Yet most of these children have experienced unimaginable traumas, having been forced to eat human flesh, to have intercourse with their mother, or to kill their own parents before the inhabitants of the village, under threat of being murdered like their little friends who could not bring themselves to do so.

Boia Efraim Junior describes three tendencies that set in progressively after such traumas.[136] Denial is the most common defense mechanism: "All I did was obey orders; othewise I would have been killed," or "Someone else would have done the same thing." The image of the atrocity is instilled in the child's memory and can re-emerge unexpectedly. If the child didn't freeze over and anesthetize the emotion associated with the memory image, no mental life would be possible. All he could to is scream in horror, as he sometimes does in the form of surprising explosions of rage. Denial enables him to keep on living to some extent, as an amputee.

Another very common defense mechanism is devaluation of the victims: "The people I killed were worthless. They were savages of an inferior race, not human at all. So what I did isn't really a crime. Sometimes it was actually a good thing, an ethnic cleansing."

Identification with the aggressor whom the child tries to surpass in cruelty is not the defense mechanism found most often out in the field. It is terrifyingly easy to observe. It is the usual mechanism of identification in schools where terrorism is taught, because here the children grow attached to the instructor and often admire him. They may proceed in the direction of sadism, in which the omnipotent child takes pleasure in the terrified expression of the man or woman he overpowers.

It is astonishing and informative to note that many such children "have managed to maintain their integrity."[137] They have tried to purify themselves through the healing rituals of their culture, have been reunited with their families, and have even returned to school.

Most observers out in the field attest to the hypermaturity of the little warriors. Almost all of these children have made intellectual progress. They speak better, discover new areas of interest, gain an awareness of politics, and improve their academic performance.[138]

Mohammed is 11 or 12 years old. Like all the very young veterans in Sierra Leone, he has probably suffered a great deal. But he will never admit this, and he may not even be conscious of it. He learned French in a few weeks' time and became an outstanding student of calculus.[139] Suffering is not the only thing that happens in a country at war. Amid all the terrifying devastation of the body and the personality, the few moments of peace and even of happiness are overinvested, and intellectual activity brings a feeling of beauty and freedom. First of all, the child feels more secure because the mere fact of understanding has an adaptive function in a hostile environment. Imminent danger leads to problems of attention, which it focuses on the aggressor, shutting out the rest of the world so that, paradoxically, intellectual performance improves.

All on-site observations made today of children at war, be it in Croatia, Kosovo, Israel, Palestine, or Timor, confirm the surprise of educators who, since the 1950s, have noted "the excellent scholastic results"[140] of children traumatized by war. A malicious reaction would be to promote war as a way of improving children's academic performance. We could try to understand the matter differently.

43. When Peace Becomes Frightening

War had prevented Edmond from attending school regularly. Two weeks here, three months there: impossible to form a bond or follow a course of study. The successive foster placements of this orphan have made him fall even further behind scholastically.

He was 10 years old when a judge placed him with a family who sent him to school, where he did abysmally. Not only did this child not know how to read and write, but he didn't even know you couldn't copy from your textbook during a test. The teacher humiliated and punished Edmond, who ran away during recess. The vicissitudes of legal decisions once again snatched him away from the beginnings of family life, returning him to the chaos of an institution.

The following year, he went back to this family, who sent him to the same school. This time, however, a new teacher was willing to form a little bond with him. As we have seen, even a small gesture on the part of another person can constitute an event for a traumatized child, and this was the first time anyone had smiled at Edmond in seven years. The teacher simply asked him to play a bit at grammar and math so as to have occasion to talk with her. Intellectual effort became a magical game, not only blurring the sadness of reality but bringing hope of an emotional relationship. School took on a different meaning for the boy. This place of imprisonment and humiliation was transformed into a wondrous space of games and encounters. Edmond awakened, and, emerging from the intellectual fog into which anxiety, despondency, and emotional isolation had plunged him, became a good student.

Most of the 300,000 child soldiers have been through a similar experience.[141] Many of them no longer know what you have to do to be a child. When all you know is how to wage war, when you don't have a family anymore, when you can't go back to your village, when, at the age of 12, you're responsible for other mutilated children, peace becomes very frightening.

How do you manage life in a country, now at peace, in which there is no emotional or cultural structure around you? This is the same situation as when children are taken from their abusive families and placed in an institution where the separation constitutes an additional traumatization. Resilience is impossible without friends, family, school, and ritualized events. So children of war regroup and discover archaic mechanisms of socialization. They form armed gangs that devastate the country or offer their services to private militias or to adults who will know how to exploit them. This phenomenon, easy to observe in all countries after a war, is now becoming evident in peacetime as well.

The upsurge in juvenile delinquency began in Europe as early as 1950. The little *suscia*, street children in starving Italy, like young Germans in their ruined country, practiced a delinquency of survival adapted to the devastation around them. Soon thereafter mindless urbanization and the creation of youth shelters that made encounters impossible led to an increase in delinquency in Austria, France, and England. This kind of delinquency did not have survival value, because these were rich countries. Nor did it arise in Portugal, which was very poor, or in Japan, which was in ruins, because these nations had maintained ritual structures organized around young people.

In Europe, improvements in urban technology facilitated the construction of crowded apartment buildings with no place for people to meet. Human interactions became more superficial.[142] In such a context, the family was no longer a place of culture and emotional shaping. Whatever claimed a child's attention came from the kids in the neighborhood. School lost its meaning. Some children evaded adult influence and submitted to the control of a gang leader.

Delinquency has increased exponentially, but misuse of statistics can give a false impression. "The number of judicial procedings against minors went from 93,000 in 1993 to 175,000 in 2000."[143] The greater ease in making allegations of aggression inflates this figure somewhat, but it is unquestionably the case that these infractions are on the rise. A very small number of minor offenders (5 percent) become "overactive" and commit the majority of thefts, attacks, drug deals, and rapes.[144] Half of these especially delinquent children are recruited in suburban housing projects, the rest from the middle-class homes surrounding the projects. Hence poverty does not determine delinquency. We should not be too quick to speak of "suburban delinquency"; this is unjust, whatever the basis in truth, since 95 percent of the people living in these areas would like to work, love, and be left the hell alone.

Yet the little groups of hyperactive and unstable young people between the ages of 13 and 18 are in fact a symptom of our society. This is not a matter of teenage rebellion against adults in the interest of discovering other modes of socializing; what we are dealing with here is a discharging of violence that was not structured by the environment.

This "violence of proximity" is learned in the first years of life as little boys insult those around them at a stage of development when they are not yet able to understand the psychological damage they are inflicting on others. As early as three years of age they hit their mother, who starts crying because "no one tells him how to behave."[145] Then, practicing discharging violence without restraint, they take on the grocer, the bus driver, and the teacher. Drunk with power, they interact only through words and blows that cause pain. Having learned nothing else, they readily form relationships of domination in which there is a leader whose insults are considered amusing and whose physical courage in stealing and brawling wins admiration. This is a delinquency of pleasure, not of survival. In this archaic form of socialization adults allow themselves to be dominated because they have not asserted their role in the shaping of their children's early development.

A small piece of information suggests a solution. At around age 19 this violence of proximity, this pleasure in discharge, often quiets down. Few young people continue to live this way when they meet someone for whom they come to feel responsible. Instead of threatening them in response to their provocations or lecturing them, which just makes them laugh, someone says, "I'm counting on you."

A relational transformation, an existential shift in direction, regularly occurs at this point. The social engagement and the emotional encounter stabilize the young person and lend meaning to his efforts. At long last, after a delay of fifteen years the law is internalized. The reparative work that begins to be offered to these young delinquents surely contributes to resilience. "From delinquency to the discovery of responsibility,"[146] reparation provides a transitional means of learning how to love and become socialized in ways other than getting pleasure from violence.

Overactive young delinquents have not suffered traumas. In fact, their material conditions are often good. But they have not acquired the conditions for resilience. There was an absence of emotional stability when they were little, they unconsciously learned relationships of domination, and they had no social circles in which to form positive substitute attachments.

I have often been surprised by the way these young people experience what they had to go through. The child soldiers would whisper that they hadn't really suffered, shrugging when their heroism was mentioned. This was not at all the case with the hedonistic delinquents who felt persecuted by the "establishment" and saw themselves as Superman.

For these two categories of young people, family and school were the major resilience factors. The child soldiers chose distant schools and were taken in by foster families so that they did not have to return to their villages, while the suburban Rambos, even when they were integrated into society, often refused to leave their neighborhoods.[147] The child soldiers were fleeing their past, but the young Rambos were afraid of new experiences.

In both cases there was a psychological catastrophe, a huge rent for the little soldiers, an absence of support that would have allowed the delinquents to construct their personhood.

44. Woe to Nations That Need Heroes

When we feel bad, when we are ashamed of ourselves, and then we suddenly find that someone else belonging to the same group shows us in a
glorious light, his success repairs us. The hero's performance mends
the altered image that others had of us. If we feel strong, happy, and
at peace, we look around for likable, available people to help us pursue our development. But if we feel weak or unjustly dominated, we'll
need a hero to represent us favorably and repair our lack of self-esteem.

I don't admire Tarzan anymore. Yet I really loved him when I was a
small, frail, dependent child. In my weakness, I believed that if I'd been
muscular I could have prevailed over nature and come to the rescue of
animals. And it was Tarzan who offered the fine, comforting public
image I aspired to, since I found security in the idea that one day I would
be as muscular, as good a swimmer, and as beloved as he was.

But as I grew older and stronger, acquiring diplomas and a bit too
much weight, I no longer felt the need for this slightly dopey and rather
colonialist muscle man. I even caught myself thinking that nowadays
Tarzan, way behind as he was in verbal skills ("Me Tarzan, you
Jane"[148]), would be sent for remedial education. No longer my hero, he
began to seem like a jerk.

I had no trouble understanding that, in the period after World War
II, adults needed heroes the way people need bandages. The film *Le Père
Tranquille* (*The Calm Father*)[149] showed a nice, average French guy. You
think he tried to avoid active combat—well, not at all; his apparent sub-
missiveness enabled him to secretly resist the army of occupation. At
exactly the same time, in 1946, the Germans were making movies about
heroes who enabled them to convince themselves that almost all of them
were anti-Nazi, the horrors having been perpetrated by just a few mur-
derers among them.[150]

Woe to those who need heroes, for they are struggling to mend themselves in imagination. This makeshift repair is a protective factor as long
as it doesn't invade the real world. Admiring Tarzan gave me the hope
that I would be like him one day, but if I had turned my back on all fam-

ily life, no longer seeking my way in society so as to become Mr. Muscle, my genitals covered with an animal skin, I would have drowned in the image that was repairing me.

This is what often happens when heroes become the saviors of vanquished nations or humiliated groups. They have a therapeutic function, but the side effects of this treatment can be very costly. A hero is never far from sacrifice, since his role is to make good a humiliation. But when the injury is a fault ("I committed a crime"; " I wasn't brave enough"; "I was conquered"), the hero becomes a redeemer who will pay for my sins. I will worship him because his glorious death repairs my image and redeems my fault, but as soon as he has paid the price I'll feel released from debt, comforted, mended, and entitled to start out anew. Then I'll have to look for other heroes to sacrifice for my greater well-being.

This crime in the name of the Good is a perverse morality, a vicarious sacrifice that repairs the survivors—for the time being. Creating heroes[151] often serves to legitimate violence: "We were just defending ourselves against the oppressor"; "They died heroes' deaths"; "They are greater dead than alive," and the like. All these graveside phrases attest to the sexualization of their violence. When the kiss of death carries them off, their triumph is even greater, since the dead are all-powerful and we don't negotiate with them.

Heroic tales always relate the same marvelous tragedy. The enemy was present everywhere, invisible, when suddenly a young man arose and smote him at the price of his own life. The hero emerged from our group, a bit above the condition of ordinary human beings, a kind of demigod. But when he saved us by feigning death, he went beyond the human condition. Did he perhaps even make a pact with the devil? What's more, when we talk to him and he tells us about the fascinating horrors he overcame, he still breathes out a few whiffs of hell. No question about it: heroes have an interest in dying if they want us to keep on loving them.

Every young person who tells himself the story of his trauma bandages himself like a hero in an exceptional situation. He must run away and save himself, and he must save others. He has been marginalized by abuse, war, incest, or a serious accident: what happened to him wasn't something ordinary, and the traumatized person can no longer be someone uninteresting. Ivan the Terrible was a peasant, but the Teutonic invasion made him into a tyrant. Little Bara, the drummer boy of the Republican Army, refused to shout "Long live the king" and was slaughtered with blows from scythes and pitchforks at age 13, but he deserves to live on for all eternity because his death glorified that army. The problem is that this kind of eternity never lasts long. Everyone has forgotten little Bara.[152] This explains why a secret army creates more heroes than a regular army that conforms too much to state regulation and is not marginal enough.

Since every humiliated group bandages itself with a hero, a traumatized, marginalized child, ashamed of what happened to him and yet feeling himself to be special, becomes eager for heroes.

45. Good for the Wounded Child Who Needs Heroes

"I don't know why I'm so quick to admire people," Gérard, age 14, told me.

"A welfare child who comes into a family is a child who brings a hidden drama along with him. . . . He may be the result of rape or incest, or the child of a prostitute. . . . He may also be the victim of abusive parents. . . . What is certain is that his parents, especially his mother, are despicable."[153] Steeped in the shame of his depraved origins, the child began to admire musicians:

"I absolutely had to make music, to find something to soothe myself. So when I was 9 I decided, without asking anyone, to make inquiries at the municipal orchestra of Le Creusot."[154] Admiring musician heroes was a way for the child to give himself a pleasant image to identify with. By becoming a musician like his heroes, he repaired the shame of being the son of someone who was "certainly despicable"—until he learned that his father was Jacques Fesch, who had been guillotined after discovering faith and was being proposed for canonization. This "discovery made it necessary for him to reconstruct himself." By bringing beauty into his life, the musician heroes had provided a treatment for the shame of his origins, lessening his pain while he was awaiting the revolution that was to "transform him from inside."[155]

The theater of heroism reveals our wounds. The revolutionaries of the nineteenth century made a hero of Bara, the little drummer boy who had dared to die for the endangered ideal of the Republic. Romand, driven into the void by his failure in medicine, made a hero of Kouchner, who had realized his dreams. Our thirst for heroes shows up our weak points, for which these people compensate when we admire them.

Shattered children need heroes as ego proxies to plant in them the hope of a reparative identification. This works the same way as our images of our parents: in childhood we worship them, in the teen years we criticize them, and in adulthood we differentiate ourselves from them even as we acknowledge their heritage. This means that all children need heroes because they feel weak. Characters in plays or comic strips enact compensatory wishes: "One day I'll be strong like him."

It also means that a shattered society doesn't offer children the same type of heroes as a peaceful one. A group of desperate people is willing to pay a high price for the sacrifice that will restore its image and redeem its mistakes. In a country at peace, on the other hand, certain heroes retain a symbolic function. Mother Teresa and Abbé Pierre have been "put there" to represent the generosity of those who are lucky enough not to suffer too much but still wish to give a little happiness to people who are in emotional or societal distress.

Conversely, a soccer player, a singer, or a princess who have become idols of the masses do not serve a reparative function. Their role is to bring poetry and dynamism, to create a splendid, luminous, and transient event in a drab society where nothing is happening. Zidane, a soccer idol for many boys, is a hero who symbolizes integration through sports for only some of them. Edith Piaf, who made an entire generation weep with the beauty of her voice, is the symbol of the integration of street children through singing only for a small minority who are familiar with her story. As for Princess Di, Louana, or the "history-making" winners of Olympic events, they are heroes with the speed of a flashbulb, showing that a culture at peace functions in the here-and-now, like a drug.

Idols are not made for purposes of representation; they are injected into the culture for its enjoyment. When a demigod no longer comes down from Olympus but is content to be seen in his Mercedes, he manufactures a kind of reality in images, as though only appearances matter. Idols are not loved for what they represent unless they are symbols; they are loved for what they incite: event, emotion, ecstasy, collective hysteria, and finally oblivion.

Heroines go through the same process. In wartime, these women repair the self-esteem of people who have been severely damaged. The Amazons, whose men disappeared, were willing to have children with foreign men, but then they killed the fathers of these children. Joan of

Arc and the Resistance heroine Lucie Aubrac attest to the participation of women in wars of liberation, and they retain this function in times of peace. Figures like Marie Curie and the aviatrix Jacqueline Auriol enable women to demonstrate their contributions to the formation of their society. But when life becomes dull and lacks identifying events, women begin to worship images. Nowadays the super-females Brigitte Bardot and Marilyn Monroe have yielded to idols with no tomorrow, women on whom to hang clothes, adored on magazine covers or in the ads that create idolatrous images.

The disintegration of our culture's heroes and their transformation into idols is a sign of peace that makes it difficult for young people to form identifications. Those who manage to see heroism in the humanitarian work of Abbé Pierre or Bernard Kouchner, or in the guerrilla warfare of Che Guevara, will be able to put themselves to the test and discover what they are worth, thereby succeeding in bringing some meaning to their lives.

But this is not true of young people who identify with paper heroes. In response to a questionnaire, high-school students of 17 and 18 mentioned seven hundred different heroes.[156] Many fictional characters and entertainment and sports figures were mentioned, along with a few scientists, writers, and scholars, but without feeling or identificatory effect. These "heroes in slippers"[157] bring about psychological mini-events as we sit in our armchairs. A sign of a society at peace, they are at the same time proof of the absence of integration in these young people with fragile identities.

War, aimed at the destruction of those who want to destroy us, and the quasi-wars of societies in the process of constructing themselves, lead to so much traumatization that the wounded groups need heroes in order to be healed. This violent integration that seeks to subjugate the other side hesitates between glory and death and often associates the two. One day we must finally invent a peacetime society that can integrate its young people and personalize them without trauma. Has our society perhaps deprived young people of rituals of integration?

46. The Anxiety of the High Diver

Adolescence in the West begins earlier and earlier and lasts longer and longer. Improved opportunities for education place a young person of 12 or 13 in the position of the diver who wonders about the height of the platform from which he will have to jump. Is there any water down there? Can his body sustain the shock? And will his soul give him the courage to hurl himself into the void?

This metaphor of the diver illustrates the attitude of an increasing number of teenagers for whom the desire to throw themselves into life is as great as the fear of jumping. The result is a kind of seething inertia in which seeking refuge in bed is never far from a sudden explosion. The kids slow down, drag school out, dream of performing a marvelous dive, and reproach society for not having put enough water in the pool and their parents for not having prepared them sufficiently. Because they feel so bad, so tensed up in this febrile rigidity, acting out has a liberating effect for them. Exploding comforts them, since, once they manage to talk about it, it helps them construct their identity: "I've been through an extraordinary event," "I'm someone who was able to make it through a dreadful ordeal."

All the ways in which we progress socially and culturally combine to develop this suffering. Advances in the understanding of early childhood, greater tolerance within the family, encouragement toward higher education, and the need to stay in school to become familiar with technological improvements—all this is in place to promote their seething inertia, not to mention the huge emotional component. Those who acquired a secure attachment in their early years may think: "I learned to love serenely. Since I'm lovable, I know I'll be loved. So I'll set about meeting the person who'll be able to love me. We'll respect and help one another."

Such young people are able to surmount the problems of adolescence. But this is not the case for the one teenager in three who acquired an insecure attachment and as a result becomes increasingly anxious when sexual desire makes its appearance.

The developmental shift to speech in the course of the third year was an extraordinary moment, the discovery of a new world that could be created solely by moving our tongue. This fabulous game improved our relationships with our attachment figures, enriching the world we shared with them as soon as we brought it to life with words. The emergence of sexual desire at the time of puberty leads to another major shift, one that is harder to negotiate because it involves relying on the emotional foundations established in the early years as we learn another way of loving. What we have to do is keep our attachment to our parent figures and yet discover that the object of our new desires calls for different kinds of behavior.

The attachment to our parents was highly differentiated sexually (a mom is most certainly not a dad) but entirely without sexual strivings. If the image of a sexual possibility had arisen, anxiety, horror, or hate would have pushed us into a violent autonomy. For the most part, when all goes well, after the crisis the adolescent retains the attachment to his parents. He then has to learn to love his partner in a different way, for she or he will have a double role to play: being the object of sexual desire and also becoming the object of an emotional bond.

The shift is hard to negotiate because we have to reconcile mixed impulses: "I engage in commitments with the imprint of my past, my idea of who I am, and the dream of my future," alongside "I have to disengage from my commitments to the people I'm still attached to. I must get free of them if I want to pursue my emotional, sexual, and social development."

The adolescent has to integrate different kinds of forces, often mutually exlusive ones. The hormonal drive activates the upsurge of sexual desire. Testosterone inflames the boys and kindles the girls, and the task now is to shape this drive. How should we express it? How should we act on it? If this gushing force is to be given an acceptable form, we have to bring our way of loving into the emotional circuits offered by our love object and our culture.

This isn't easy in the best of circumstances. Thus it's clear that, if one of the partners has had problems with emotional development or the culture provides no model for loving behavior, the process will be even harder. When an early relational deficit has not been corrected in the family sphere in the course of day-to-day interactions, the emotional problem becomes acute during adolescence.

Paradoxically enough, the problems are easier to deal with when they are visible. We can help a child change his attachment pattern and teach him to love in a more agreeable way. This probably explains why, in a long-term follow-up of a group of children who learned a style of insecure (ambivalent, avoidant, or confused) attachment early on, we observe that one third of them will make a surprising improvement in adolescence and acquire a secure attachment.[158]

47. Even the Sturdiest Are Afraid to Take the Plunge

In contrast, we are surprised to note that one fourth of children with unproblematical attachment will break down in adolescence and become insecure. We were probably unable to discern the invisible problems of attachment. Children who are too good, too well adjusted, please adults or rather reassure them. When children are too well behaved, adults lavish less attention on them, and the result is a phobic equivalent, an excessive attachment on the part of the child who does not dare to strike out on his own and therefore flatters the adult by being too obedient.

Overprotected children seem to flourish serenely because they have never had the opportunity to test themselves. We think of them as solid because they have never revealed their weakness, until the day when some minor event devastates them. Then they reproach their stunned parents for not having equipped them for life, which is unfair to these devoted parents but not incorrect. Not to mention the fact that these abnormally well-balanced children, shored up by a constantly attentive environment, mask their fearfulness by readily obeying. In adolescence they experience their past relationship as a submission, rebelling against parental influence in explosions of hate.

There are, of course, totalitarian families in which a parent imposes his or her concept of life on the whole household and manages to control all aspects of personal life. Children growing up in these family groups are strongly shaped by the authoritarian context. They adjust to it because they can't do otherwise without risking expulsion.

What flares up in adolescence, leading to either blossoming or collapse, is the mode of attachment established early on. We can therefore try to predict what kind of teenagers abused children will become. At the age of 18 months, 75 percent of abused children exhibit altered modes of attachment (as opposed to 35 percent of the general population).[159] The intensity of the problems varies, but on the whole these babies are highly avoidant, do not maintain eye contact, do not respond to a smile, and react only faintly to information not at close range. Most seriously affected are surely children who have been neglected or abandoned, sometimes even left alone in a room or closet for weeks or months at a time. Dazed and confused, they are terrified by any stimulation, especially affectionate appeals, which often give rise to self-injury.

Just as a group of children who have formed a serene attachment will retain this style of connectedness until adolescence, when only one in four will have trouble making the shift, a group of children with troubled attachment will exhibit unstable emotional styles. In such cases, the mode of attachment depends on the interaction with the person encountered. Most neglected children come back to emotional warmth, but the progress of the recovery varies according to the two people involved. Some children warm up again right from the first months of interaction with parental substitutes who are sometimes not very available emotionally, while others come back to life slowly. Emotional transactions are easier with a couple than with one other person, which does not mean that they are more intense. This leads to the conclusion that, although deprived children must be loved in order to provide them with some underpinnings of resilience, there is no relation between the dosage and the effects. Children who are loved more and more will not reestablish themselves better and better. But if they are not loved, their future is easy to predict: their development will stop.

It is hard to deprive a child of affection entirely, short of putting him in a closet or leaving him alone at home with a fridge and a TV. We may wonder why, in the case of serious deprivation, only 75 percent of children are affected. Why not 100 percent? Because, around the deficient or abusive mother, there was a husband, a grandparent, a neighbor, or an institution that offered some underpinnings of resilience. When there is a monopoly on influences and the child cannot escape and meet up with other means of support, when an environment has been turned to stone by the domination of a single person, when this emotional control is authoritarian, the sensory surround, the behaviors, the gestures, and the words will always be the same, and the child will remain their prisoner. One and the same enveloping structure of abuse or emotional stifling will not have the same effects if the child can find an opening, and that may be enough.

Lisa was very frightened of her father, who used to beat her every night and would often even run after her with a sword to make her think he was going to kill her. Luckily, every afternoon between the time she left school and the time her father got home, Lisa was able to slip off to a neighbor's house to run some errands for her, tidy up a bit, and look after her baby. Each evening's torment became a mere puff of air from hell, because, just before, Lisa had experienced an adult-like period of time during which she was able to show herself capable of strong, generous relationships.

As the nightmare drew near, she would hold onto the belief that a just and affectionate world could exist if only she went and looked for it, which she has done all her life. From adolescence on, as soon as she was able to leave, she discovered her talent for finding men, women friends, groups, countries, and languages where affection and plans can be shared. The adultism that was a costly defense during her childhood became a resilience factor when she was able to change her environment. Today she runs a business, speaks five languages, and lives in ten countries surrounded by numerous friends. Her neighbor will never know how much she protected Lisa by enabling her to prove to herself that there are other kinds of life than her family's and to come to believe that she was capable of them.

When a family milieu is deficient, a neighborhood structure, the way of life in a town, or the creation of professional networks of art, sports, or psychology are enough to sow the seed of a process of resilience. Gaining a serene attachment can occur in places other than one's family.[160] But for that to happen the culture must provide openings and stop thinking in terms of univocal relationships in which a single cause leads to a single effect.[161]

The young person preparing to negotiate the shift into adolescence undertakes this difficult and exciting test with the self-concept he has formed in the course of his life. In the moment when Lisa was fleeing from her sword-wielding father, she was exhibiting an adaptive run-for-your-life tactic and not a mechanism of resilience. It was only later, as she represented this event to herself, that she was able to say proudly, "Now that I've escaped, I've won my freedom, and all I have to do is build the life that suits me. What means are available to me in my personal life and my environment?"

It is with a collage of small victories that the young person undertakes the shift into adolescence. Driven by the surge of sexual desire that forces him to leave his family, he takes stock of the successes that legitimize his belief in his abilities and in a just world. This comes down to saying that a young person imprisoned in his past by an abusive memory, immured in a closed or authoritarian family, deprived of small victories by an all-too-devoted group of people, or living in a weakly structured society will have a hard time becoming resilient.

48. Belief in a Just World Brings Hope of Resilience

This feeling that the world is just is rather surprising when we know just what these beaten, raped, banished, and exploited children have been through. This is because the phrase "belief in a just world" refers to two attitudes that are antithetical to one another and yet both contribute to resilience.

The first of these attitudes consists in saying, "I was an innocent victim, but I can pull through because the new world that's welcoming me is a just world." This is something like the ideology of popular novels in the nineteenth century, in which Oliver Twist, Rémi, and Cosette, deserving children severely damaged by wicked adults, blossom forth again as soon as they find a middle-class family or the right social group. These edifying novels give renewed hope to those whose souls have been wounded, encouraging them to adjust to society and take their place there.

In contrast, the other belief in a just world calls for a rebellion: "I was beaten, expelled from school, kept from finding a place in society, imprisoned, or deported. And yet there is such a thing as a just world; all we have to do is destroy this society and replace it with that of the thinker, priest, or friend I believe in."

Both visions of the world invite us to take action in order to find a place in a just society, present or future.

These schemas cover those former welfare children who have become CEOs or rich captains of industry[162] as well as the street children who grew up to be innovators. Takano Masao, orphaned by the struggle between Japan and Korea in the 1940s, survived in the street by dint of bartering and begging: "I recall living without any feelings. Sadness, joy, and pain were completely unknown to me. . . . The cops treated us as hoodlums or rejects and told us to hurry up and die because we were parasites in society."[163]

A single encounter tipped his fate in the opposite direction. When he was starving to death in Tamahine Park, where Tokyo's outcasts were dumped, a ragpicker gave him a bowl of noodles mixed with dog offal.

He came back to life, and, in order to establish a bond with this man, decided to learn how to read, something the ragpicker could do. During the day, the child worked in the street to pay for night school (as is still done today in the Philippines).

In November 1966, such evening courses were discontinued because child labor was declared illegal. Takano Masao undertook to fight on behalf of children and was successful in keeping thirty-four night schools going. "All of them without exception were filled with orphans of Japanese, Chinese, . . . [and] Korean nationality, . . . refugees from Southeast Asia, and Brazilians who had come to Japan to work." In a Western context this educational arrangement would be considered a form of mistreatment, but in the context of cultural breakdown, begging and night school became supports for resilience.

The way a fact is spoken of in a child's milieu is what determines whether it is destructive or reconstructive. In a stable society where the narratives convey the belief that everyone has a fixed place in a hierarchy, any act of aggression can be justified: "Odd how some people are always victims. She just got what she deserved! It was no accident." The mental impossibility of challenging the very notion of hierarchy keeps witnesses to the attack from trying to help the injured. In order to avoid feeling guilty, they even tend to devalue the victim[164]: "Women who were raped must have been looking for it," "Abandoned children must have been born brain damaged or autistic," "Delinquents must have come from a background of poverty." Order reigns.

49. Can a Victim Be Made Into a Cultural Star?

Cultural stereotypes have been shifting over the past few decades. Nowadays we prefer to identify with the victim. In fact, we almost tend to regard him as an initiate because he has had a brush with death: he has something to teach us about the invisible world from which he has come back as a ghost. We encourage him to speak and sometimes, when what he says corresponds to social expectations, even make him into a cultural star. And this leads people to come forth with highly plausible, but false, claims of victimization.

Binjamin Wilkomirski wrote a little book called *Fragments*, in which he tells about his Polish childhood "in various children's barracks of the camps where the Nazis imprisoned Jews."[165] When he describes Auschwitz and how his adoptive father handed him over to Mengele, the doctor who tortured prisoners in medical experiments, the account is so impressive, so close to the expected clichés, that it acquires mythological truth. Its horrible beauty is part of the esthetic of the charnel house that is very appealing to a society of overconsumption. A few images are enough to create the sense of an event. We talk about it, are moved and indignant, run to the rescue, and give ourselves the right to attack the attacker. Then, at last, we feel good. Something lovely happened, an existential moment in our boring life. We had to see, understand, read, talk, meet, and join together to prevent such atrocities. We feel beautiful in the face of such ugliness, generous in the face of injustices, brave in the face of monsters. We normal people need the horror endured by victims so that our personal grandeur can shine forth.

Binjamin "Wilko" speaks with a Yiddish accent, is phobic about trains since they remind him of deportation, and constantly moves his feet in order, he says, to chase away the rats that used to run all over him in the camps. Actual survivors immediately spotted the accumulation of clichés. But clichés have power only because they correspond to the gluttony of normal people who take delight in Holocaust kitsch. If you experienced what Auschwitz was like, you suffered, of course, but

that was not all. You also encountered a moment of friendship or a flash
of beauty that made the unbearable bearable.

The suffering changed form after the war, when speaking about it
met with incredulity or moralizing on the part of the liberators:
"What! You ate garbage? You're pigs!" said the generous Americans,
who didn't know that *Schwein* ("pig") was the Nazis' preferred insult.
When "an account is normalized, agreed upon, [it becomes] a largely
instrumentalized litany. Memory has become formatted in the direction of what passes for popular wisdom."[166]

This is why the relatives of survivors were happy to accept
Wilkomirski's horrible fairy tale: it corresponded to their notion of
reality. And, of course, a personal account is always more moving,
beautiful, and convincing than an official report.

The cultural attitude most conducive to the development of individual resilience is one that avoids extremes. Belittling a victim to
shore up the established order does not lead to a better result than
putting him onstage for our enjoyment. But "ever since the 1980s special attention has been paid to victims by the powers that be."[167] Once
his status is acknowledged, the victim can exist in society as he would
after an accident. He can then become "devictimized" by working on
his resilience.[168]

50. How to Rewarm a Frozen Child

Throughout our lives we become involved in events with the resources imprinted in us by our personal history. When you spend decades dealing with abused children, you observe that they undertake their first romantic relationship with all the pain their past has taught them but also with constructive defenses.

For the most part, such children are highly vulnerable to any emotional loss, having had no opportunity to learn how to hope for love or get over disappointment. They keep safe by avoiding love and then are very sad on account of this lack.[169] They suffer less, but that's all.

Several subgroups can be observed in this population of children with avoidant attachment. One set of sixty-two abused children was followed from preschool, to regular school, and then to the institutions in which they were placed.[170] About a third had been physically assaulted. In preschool, after a short period of keeping to themselves and hesitating to join the group, they finally joined the others very confidently, even a bit aggressively. Children who had been verbally assaulted found it harder to integrate. They remained inhibited and confused for a long time, avoiding interaction with their peers or responding in a puzzling way that was hard to decipher. This behavior, learned at home and later expressed in preschool and regular school, decreased their chances of finding a little friend who might have provided support for resilience.

The third group consisted of neglected children. For a variety of reasons (for example, the mother was very young, poor, and alone) these children found themselves in a situation like that of the sensory isolation in some experiments with animals: no contact, no facial expressions, no words or games, and minimal, perfunctory care. This was the most seriously affected group. Up to age 6 they exhibited a great deal of withdrawal behavior, with frozen emotions, no games, no creativity, many signs of insecurity (for example, covering their heads with their arms at the slightest noise), marked retardation in gestures and speech, and passivity in the face of small aggressions by their peers.

Parental neglect "seems to have the most devastating effects on the child's socio-emotional and cognitive development."[171] Yet there are still small embers of resilience: this is the group in which we have observed several adultist scenarios, as though these neglected children had tried to preserve a bond by taking care of the maltreating parent.

It may be the case, then, that the form of mistreatment organizes a sensory environment around the child that selectively promotes a particular type of problem and a particular type of resilience. All the children are affected, but the ways in which this occurs and the strategies of resilience seem to differ. Physically abused children develop an emotional intensity that will be hard for them to control once they reach adolescence. Yet they reach out toward others in a way that fosters socialization later on. Verbally abused children are the humiliated ones whose self-esteem has been crushed. Yet it is in this group that we find the most imaginative, mythic, or heroic forms of resilience. Devastation is greatest among the neglected children, and they have the fewest constructive defenses. The exception is when an adultist interaction is still possible with a negligent but childlike grown-up.

When we study this problem we have to assemble separate clinical cohorts (physical abuse, verbal abuse, negligence). But in the spontaneous human adventure, these distinctions are seldom clear, since it is not unusual to find a child who is insulted while being hit and is then locked in the cellar. A spontaneous situation may highlight an important ember of resilience: the plasticity of the child's responses.

Hans was 2 when his father disappeared in wartime. His mother withdrew emotionally, and, after the warmth of his environment up to that time, the child had to survive despite her negligence. But Hans had already acquired a serene attachment. He kept on reaching out to his inert mother until she had to be hospitalized and eventually disappeared as well.

Orphaned at 4, in the course of the following years Hans was placed in a variety of institutions amid the social breakdown of postwar Germany. As a teenager, when he looked back on his life he was surprised at the different clinical pictures he presented in these different settings. At first he had numbed himself because he was suffering so much and because no adult had the time to talk to him. Yet in this emotional desert a few sparks of resilience enabled him to hold onto hope. In Essen, a "monitor" who was in charge of forty children gathered them together every evening and told them exciting war stories.

This heroic boasting might have seemed obscene to an observer in peacetime, but it meant a lot to Hans, who could at last picture his father dying nobly in defense of his country. Before this, having seen gaping, stinking, and rotting corpses in the mud, the child had tried not to think about his father's death.

Some sort of administrative decision then sent him to Erfurth, where a thousand children had been brought together in a castle. Here a few overburdened adults spent their time keeping the accounts and searching for food. In the absence of supervision, a gang of little burglars between the ages of 10 and 14 imposed their own law. Hans hung around with them but did not admire them. He, too, became a bit of a bruiser and a thief and was quite proud of having dug a tunnel under the wire fence surrounding the property. He knew how to slip into the staff store at night through a broken window. Selling the stolen goods in the street the next day was a source of amusing adventures, good business deals, and frantic escapes.

When his fellow delinquents were arrested and sent to another institution, Hans managed to escape capture. But his petty crimes stopped that very day. When he thought about it, he said to himself that if he had been caught, he would have probably been labeled "delinquent" and that this term, imposed from outside, would have become part of his identity.

51. Learning to Love Despite Abuse

Hans was surprised at how attracted he was to girls. From the time he was 4, before any sexual appetite, simply being close to a little girl gave him a great sense of peace and happiness. Their prettiness, graceful gestures, and fondness for talking suited Hans, who did his best to be in their company. But girls' games bored him; he preferred the races, fights, ongoing rivalries, and constantly negotiable rules of the boys. Yet, as soon as the match was over, he'd go over to a girl and move into a different emotional world.

One Sunday, when the children had each been given a piece of sponge cake for dessert, Hans stole the portion belonging to an older boy, who chased Hans across the yard for a long time and punched him in the face. Hans was still groggy when a little girl left the group and came over to console him with kind words. On that day he discovered the pleasure of interpersonal warmth, the price he was willing to pay to get some of it, and the importance of his own emotional life. Highly dependent on the least sign from the "monitors," who could enchant or hurt him with a single word, he figured out how much affection matters.

It was with this kind of past shaping, this emotional apprenticeship, that Hans undertook the shift into adolescence. The thrilling and stunning incursions of sexual desire called upon everything he had learned since early childhood and would now have to be expressed in his sexual involvements.

The feelings a boy has when associating with girls before the emergence of sexuality are not at all the same as when he can say to himself, "All I have to do is look at them and a delicious feeling comes over me. Women mean something else to me now. I like this new perception a lot, because I've learned to give form to my emotions and because adults have helped me by offering cultural models."

But the same budding sensation can lead to anxiety in those whose past has instilled an uncontrollable turmoil in them. Young people in this group turn to their customary defenses against inner distress: "I'll hold back and become rigid to keep from exploding. I can also tell myself that what I'm feeling in my body is an illness, which makes me less anxious than thinking in terms of a sex drive that could carry me away who knows where. I can also get aggressive, because aggression can often be a way to conceal fear."

The myriad forms that the beginnings of love can take always lead to major changes. Some teenagers calm down, blossom, and make a start on a life plan, while others grow anxious and some break down, destroyed by an unbearable passion.

To gain a better understanding of such different outcomes, two groups of children between 12 and 18 months were studied. The development of the group with secure attachment was compared with that of the group with insecure attachment. The children were seen again twenty years later in a semi-structured interview that invited them to tell about their first romantic experience.[172] Their tape-recorded accounts were then submitted to a linguist for semantic analysis.

By definition, the first love affair ends badly. (Since it's the first, it can't have lasted.) The overwhelming majority of those with serene attachment described this event with words like "happy," "friendly," "trusting," "having ups and downs," "not too painful," and "tenderness." For no apparent reason, 18 percent of the young people fell apart at that moment.

In the group with insecure attachment, the first love affair was described with words like "pain," "jealousy," "sadness," and "unpleasant." But 28 percent got over it surprisingly well.

Most of those with serene attachment went into the first love affair with an emotional style that made them attentive to the other person but without surrendering to the experience, losing a sense of self, or "experiencing love as a trauma."[173] The lightness of the connection made it possible for them not to be engulfed by the moment of love or feel depleted by the separation. In euphoria and sadness alike, they remained themselves.

Most of those with insecure attachment were hurt by the first encounter. Romantic ecstasy gave rise to an anxious dilemma they found it hard to put into words: "It's wonderful; I love her. It's terrifying; I'm going to lose her. In order to keep her, I have to lose myself in her. She's destroyed my sense of myself, so I hate her." (Similar feelings would, of course, hold true for a woman's experience.)

Teenagers with secure attachment even profited from the test of their first love affair so as to improve their relationship the next time around: "I'll be able to love better. Yes, you have to be able to give, but without losing what you have." In contrast, those with insecure attachment, wounded by their first love, often learned to be afraid of loving. For many of them, the abundance of loving feelings changed into a fascination with death. Forty-five percent of teenagers dead by suicide had lost a parent early in life, either through death or after a divorce.

Emotional vulnerability that set in very early on was often masked in later childhood by overseriousness, an inability to take things lightly. For the most part, behavior that might have revealed this vulnerability was misinterpreted by teachers. When a child becomes a good student because he feels anxious the minute he lifts his nose from his textbook, he will be considered studious. When he stays glued to his parents, billing and cooing with them all the time and covering them with presents, he is described as very affectionate, whereas in fact this is an anxious overattachment in which he is trying to love his parents as fast as possible before their imminent death. In this way, the loving intensity that reveals these components of the personality reveals weak points and leads to breakdown.

52. Mending After Being Torn

We now have to ask why it is that the loss of a parent early on through death or divorce can lead to a vulnerability that, twenty years later, will make some adolescents in love fall apart while others, in exactly the same circumstances, will experience the romantic encounter as shoring up their personality, as a powerful support for resilience.

Death and divorce are such landmark events that some studies were too quick to blame them for a child's vulnerability. Later work has clearly shown that the guilt aroused by these events is what causes the crack in the child's personality that will become a break later on. If he finds suitable substitutes, he will continue developing harmoniously. The day will come, however, when his environment informs him of the cultural stereotypes according to which an orphan or child of divorce must be in great pain. Then the young person will be ashamed of his sense of well-being and, when he falls in love for the first time, will try to prove that he is not a monster by being too nice, too focused on the other person.

At that point the depersonalizing or, on the contrary, sustaining effect of this first love affair will depend on the partner's own personality and history. He may take advantage of the excessive devotion of the adolescent who has not completed the mourning process, drag her down, sacrifice her to his own needs, and then scorn her for having been a pushover. The first love affair has a taste of bitterness. "After all I did for him (or her), I got taken for a ride," these boys and girls say, unhappy because they gave so much, bitter because they were swindled emotionally even though, unconsciously, they were candidates for just that.

Or the partner may be delighted to find such a devoted lover. He doesn't know that she, too, is surprised that someone is willing to offer love. He doesn't know that her instability has been "cured" by the emotional security he has been providing for her. The wounded adolescent's sensitive phase is then followed by a successful shift to resilience. In such cases, the coming together of two vulnerabilities has strengthened the couple.

What makes a bereaved child feel guilty is that the conflictual relationship his parents established before they died was a poor setting for
his development. Later on, what substitute families and the culture say
about this death—that it was heroic or shameful, deserved or unjust—
will soothe or exacerbate that feeling of guilt. Every wounded young
person finds himself at the center of a constellation of influences that he
must constantly deal with.

We can understand the effects of divorce with a similar argument. It
is not the parents' separation that causes the injury but the emotional
charge associated with it. When the father is sent abroad on a socially
valued mission, when the mother has to be away in order to fulfill her
intellectual or artistic talent, older children experience this separation
as a glorious challenge. But when the parents are devastated because
they feel obliged to stay home in the company of their intimate enemy,
they are not better supports for their child's resilience than parents who
have come to terms with separation and, in spite of everything, offer a
modified environment for their children's development.

Separation as such is not a major factor, except for a baby who lives
in the here and now and needs a constant presence. For an older child,
the social context and sequence of events are what give the event its
meaning. A separation may be experienced as a little adventure, or, in
the opposite case, the child may suffer when he has been steeped in hate
or when subsequent events cause the separation to be associated with
loss or guilt. If the mother forms a new relationship immediately after
the divorce, this harms the child more than if the father does so. This is
because divorce almost always occurs when the child is between 6 and
10 and has not yet acquired full emotional autonomy, and because the
attachment to the mother is not of the same kind as to the father.

What harms a child and sets him up for experiencing his first love
affair as painful is not the spectacular event of his parent's divorce but
the insidious sense of rejection. Such children find it impossible to form
an emotional bond that feels safe; they live with the fear of imminent
separation and the anxiety of loss. It is in this population that we find
the largest number of invisible traumas.

These blows are often inflicted when no witnesses are present. It is not uncommon for parents to say things like: "I'm sorry you didn't die the day you were born," "It would have been better if the doctor hadn't tried to resuscitate you," or "I wish you were the one who died, not your little brother." Since such things are said in private, no correctives were forthcoming from the environment: "It wasn't all that bad," "Mommy's just upset." The child lives with that remark in his memory and tacks it onto the least little daily event. Whenever his mother is late picking him up at school, he thinks, "She's going to abandon me." Every comment like, "You've got a sore throat again" means "She hopes I'll die from it." Each such minor event keeps the rupture going and hinders the acquisition of internal resources of resilience. And, since the aggression was private, there are no external resources either. Everything is in place for trauma, and observers will say, "It's hard to understand why a delightful challenge like a first flirtation did such damage. She's really very fragile."

One of every five children who attempt suicide witnessed the murder or suicide of one of his parents.[174] He entered adolescence with the idea that an unhappy love affair could be a reason for death, because, in his earlier years, he was unable to learn hope, the internal resource of resilience. For him, it's love or death.

53. It Is Up to the Culture to Blow on the Embers of Resilience

I have never heard about a more difficult childhood than Juliette's. Her mother had wanted to die when giving birth to her, and her desperation at having a child was so great that she neglected the baby for several months. Inert, immobile, staring up at the ceiling, Juliette wasn't dead. But she wasn't alive, either, and finally the doctor had to put her in the hospital so she could be revived.

After spending time in various institutions, since her mother was better and since, at that time, the ideology of maternal bonding prevented any thought of separation, the child was returned to the home. For several years Juliette grew up in an emotional setting in which the mother was isolated, worn out, silent, mechanical, and subject to sudden outbursts of violence against herself in which she would bang her head against the wall, scream in despair, or cut her wrists in front of the child.

Fascinated by this gloomy and explosive love object, little Juliette couldn't interest herself in anything besides her mother, toward whom she displayed an anxious attachment. And so she felt torn apart when she was placed with a nursemaid, crying day and night and rejecting whatever came from this woman. The nursemaid soon began to hate the child and revealed a previously hidden sadism. She would tie Juliette to a chair and beat her, taking a long time to prepare her blows in order to terrify the child; then, to relax, she would go for a walk after carrying the child, still bound to the chair, into the dark cellar.

From time to time, Juliette would go to school, where she was made fun of. She was attacked because she was dirty, smelly, had a shaved head, and was badly dressed, her shoes having practically no soles. Sitting dully in a corner, she felt like an idiot on account of the difficulty she had understanding what the others seemed to find easy. At age 14, she was caught by four tramps and taken to a hovel where she was repeatedly raped and beaten. When she returned to the nursemaid she was beaten again for being late.

It is with this history that she reached adolescence. She would run away, sleep in squats, and insult everyone who tried to help her. And

yet there were a few embers of resilience: a mad dream, completely il-
logical, almost delusional given how far it was from being able to be
fulfilled. Juliette would feel better when she sat in a corner and dreamed
like crazy of cooking dinner while waiting for a nice husband to come
home from work. She also had a daydream she considered less romantic, in which she grew very big and strong, went back to the nursemaid,
and scalped her.

In a hostel near Nice she was taught to wash, dress correctly, and
express her opinions in ways other than fighting. A pretty girl who always clowned around, she attracted several boys. So she fell in love,
dreamed of getting married in white, made progress in learning to cook,
and showed her love by holding onto her boyfriend's every gesture and
moment. He was nice enough to let her take him over and gave her two
children, a boy and a girl, until she threw him out because he had spent
too much time talking with another woman.

Juliette was surprised to find how much she detested her daughter,
who reminded her of her nursemaid. She constantly rebuffed her but
would have felt ashamed to beat her. As for the boy, from the age of 6
on he assumed responsibility for his mother. He would kiss her when
she was sad and bring her cookies when she took refuge in bed. She
felt much better when he did well in school. "His success made me feel
worthwhile," she said. The girl, feeling rejected, left home at a very
young age, as did the boy, who preferred to continue growing up
without having to dedicate himself to consoling his mother.

Today Juliette lives alone in a room where the shutters are always
closed, earning her living by keeping house for elderly people, the only
ones with whom she feels at peace.

No one blew on an ember of resilience. When she was a baby, the
ideology of the maternal bond returned her to a mother who was too
weak to take care of her. Instead of being subjected to a sadistic nursemaid, she could have been placed in children's groups led by instructors with various talents (art, sports, speech), who could have taught
her to use her sense of humor as a relational strength. Her beauty, too,
was a resilience factor, unfair but usable. Good grooming, putting on

makeup, and dressing well lets you express your inner self outwardly on your body and prepares you for verbal and emotional dialogues. Since she was surprised at how possessive her way of loving was, a novel, a film, or a play might have been enough to raise the problems of her controlling relationship, her hatred for her daughter, or her son's adultism. She might then have turned out differently.

The culture of the time offered her no support for resilience. It was only at the price of a major amputation of her existence that she became able to suffer less.

Juliette's story shows how the first knots of resilience could have been tied at each stage of the construction of her personality, but this would have taken a different form each time: sensory for a baby to induce familiarity; pictorial later on to outline a stable attachment figure; relational in school to set in motion the pleasure of exploring new things; sexual and social at the time of adolescence when the young person takes stock of the inner capital that he has accumulated in the past and now seeks to invest so as best to advance his future interests.

The number of neglected children seems to be increasing rapidly in our culture. This kind of mistreatment is hard to observe, since the children aren't beaten, raped, or abandoned. Yet the absence of emotional and social structure in the child's environment leads to developmental changes. Because emotional control is poorly learned, attachment figures who might provide safety are not recognized, and each novelty evokes fear instead of pleasure. So it is no surprise that, in adolescence, the intensity of sexual desire and the enormous challenge of the social adventure cause panic and not sweet daydreams.

54. Taking Risks so as Not to Think

The usual adaptive defense in these neglected children is self-soothing through emotional numbness and through the creation of a self-centered world. This is the capital with which they make the shift into adolescence. Never having known support, they haven't had the opportunity to learn how to rely on others and hence to ask for help. Neglected babies destroy themselves by wasting away; isolated orphans are made so anxious by emotional contact that they let themselves sink into the water when they are being bathed or go limp on the floor when someone wants to take care of them. Older children with emotional deficits in their upbringing stomp on gifts they are given or immediately forget them.

When the fire of adolescence is kindled any encounter brings on a crisis. Speaking kindly to them throws them into despair. Teenagers who have had enough emotional and social support throw themselves into this adventure with joyous excitement. Should there be a minor disappointment, they manage to regard it as a learning experience. This is not the case with children with developmental deficits, for whom every choice is a crisis: "The sexuality I want makes me terribly anxious. How could a woman possibly want me? If she gets pregnant or just wants to be in a relationship with me, I'm prepared to be a slave to this woman I don't love, because staying alone would make me feel desperate. Solitary sex makes me feel desperate, and meeting someone, which I want so much, makes me feel anxious."

The emergence of sexual desire has triggered panic. Many teenagers suffer from this panic and find vaguely adaptive solutions like running away, copping out, inhibition, aggression caused by fear, or looking for someone guilty to sacrifice. But practically all those who have discovered the process of resilience have made risk manageable, which gives them a sense of triumph.

It is often during this sensitive stage that life stories become organized around certain themes. "The only events I can deal with are intense ones," these young people may say. They willingly make themselves prisoners of context, since physical and emotional intensity prevents them from dwelling on their past and fearing their future. They put themselves into situations where they are tested so that the risk of reality will keep them from the risk of thinking.[175] The teenager feels better. This defense blinds him, as he wishes it to, and if he emerges victorious, as he hopes, he will have constructed a bit of his identity, since, after the event, he will finally have something to say.

For a teenager, what is at issue is not so much taking a risk as an adventure in identification enabling him to discover what he wants. And it is surely a kind of initiation that he is staging, not a death wish: "I'd definitely commit suicide," a sweet girl told me, "but I'm afraid I'd regret it afterwards." The search for a sense of emergency is a protective factor close to denial: "Look, I don't have time now. We'll deal with it later," say those young people who feel better when the constraint of reality enables them to escape self-representations. But they themselves are imposing this violence: "I've been working twenty hours a day getting ready for this exam. I'm exhausted, and yet I feel better because this intensity gives me hope of success and keeps me from thinking about my family relationships, which are one long misery."

Those with secure attachments find it easier to round the cape of adolescence. The great majority of them accept sexuality and social engagement as challenges they overcome with the strange, fearful pleasure they get from driving too fast or screaming on a ferris wheel. This is why 75 percent of such young people maintain secure attachments when circumstances become adverse. Needing to feel safe, in a difficult situation they will phone their attachment figures, make an effort to have friends around them, or slip into a regression that calms them down. But a secure attachment isn't a guarantee for life. It simply facilitates the subsequent stage of development and enables the adolescent to maintain internal stability with positive defenses during the turmoil of this period.[176]

Yet 25 percent of them will go under during this shift. They seem to be the ones who have developed well and securely but have lacked challenges, and hence triumphs, in the course of their lives.

55. Cultural Signposts for Taking Risk: Initiation

For adolescents who have developed well, any confrontation amounts to an initiation. As for those whose education has been disastrous, they have no choice: the trauma is there, it is real, and it must be faced. But it takes on the value of an initiation for young people who refuse to stay wounded all their lives. The reason this can happen is that almost one traumatized teenager in three will, without intending to, change his attachment style and become untroubled in adolescence.[177] This figure can be improved when we understand what enables these wounded children to blossom as adolescents. Two words characterize this favorable course: *thematization* and *opening*.

First, thematization. These surprising adolescents stopped suffering from their trauma as soon as they gave it meaning: "I want to understand how a mistreated child can escape repeating the mistreatment." Theorization is often a defensive act, but when research transforms the meaning of the trauma, it gives meaning to the life of the seeker, the former wounded child: "I want to campaign to prevent another civil war in Rwanda."[178] "I can't bear to see a country sending its army to occupy another country, since I lived through that in Poland."[179] By giving a theme to the wounded person's life, trauma changes the meaning of that life, becoming a means of struggle and not a weakening.

Second, opening. Even for an adolescent who has developed well, disengagement is necessary. He must find a sexual partner outside his family of origin and form a new bond with him or her to escape the suffocation of an incestuous climate. But a number of different kinds of forces have to come together to make this disengagement possible.

The teenager must erotize exploration if he is not to remain a prisoner of his family. In addition, the culture must offer him places and opportunities for disengagement. Almost all abused children who have become untroubled in adolescence found an opportunity for early autonomy and did so sooner than their peers.[180] If the teenager is afraid of the world and the culture does not invite him to venture out, he will remain stuck in his family and be unable to separate. In a group of mistreated children who have managed to settle down, we often find an appeal to the beauty that the culture has made available: "Notre-Dame is my chapel. The Seine holds me. My history flows between its banks. When I am close to those banks I'm not afraid of anything."[181] To this external resilience factor must be added an internal one, the reaching out to others that makes encounters possible: "People in love possess wealth. . . . I grew up in hell with the certainty of being privileged."

So here we have the problem. Trauma is a rupture that, for the resilient, ultimately has the effect of an initiation. Seventy-five percent of young people with secure attachment undertake the shift into adolescence without too much suffering and maintain this protective style. They experience the first love affair, the first departure, the first job as a difficulty from which they can learn something, a delightful test. But 33 percent of those with insecure attachment will profit from these tests by gaining autonomy and learning to love in a pleasant way.[182] No teenager in these flourishing groups has escaped problems, and some, after the traumas of childhood, have even managed to triumph over the difficulties of adolescence.

As one might expect, 70 percent of those with insecure attachment do not successfully negotiate the shift. Their withdrawal from engagement, shame about their origins, fear of society, and emotional failures have set them in the direction of a difficult life. But, as one might not have expected, 25 percent of those with untroubled attachment became frozen, avoidant, ambivalent, or disoriented in adolescence. This was probably a matter of false secure attachments: children who appeared loving because they were anxious. Their great serenity expressed a lack of joy in life, and their good scholastic results were evidence not of a fondness for school but of fear of the teachers.

Another surprise was the observation that when all the child's needs were satisfied, when he was kept from having to face the slightest challenge, stuffed full of love, and bound in a net of protectiveness, he could not acquire the resources necessary for resilience.[183]

The adolescent shift is a critical moment in which much is at stake. Insofar as trauma is a psychological intrusion that forces change on those who continue to live despite the bruising, all adolescence is a dangerous shift.

What is more, these young people often feel the need to stage a brush or flirtation with death. Their erotization of violence is not a "need for trauma"[184] but an appetite for life. Such an event is a form of initiation because there must be a first time, and so the teenagers are impelled to use whatever their culture makes available to them and make an initiatory rite out of it. But when the culture no longer organizes such a rite, they invent one that is barbaric; risky driving, unprotected sex, drugs, delinquency, dangerous pastimes, and difficult journeys take on a stimulating effect that promotes identity and integration: "Something is finally happening in my life. There will be outstanding events in my history. I've come a long way. From now on I can occupy a responsible sexual place among adults."

Here we find a kind of natural resilience: "I need to discover what I'm worth by confronting the world in such a way that I give form to who I am by telling my story and understand what I'm aspiring to as I dream of my future. I intellectualize, I dramatize, I globalize my challenges, I make commitments, I love, I shock, I make people laugh." The line between natural resilience and the resilience of traumatized adolescents who have been initiated despite themselves is a narrow one. The latter have come close to death, they have tricked it; some have stayed in hell while others have returned from hell . . . resilient.

Adolescence forces change. Puberty alters the body, desire turns the emotions inside out, emotional encounters rework parental attachments, and social aspirations lead to new relationships. Even those teenagers who flourish don't escape these changes. Their family and culture have made directional circuits available to them, railroad tracks as it were, suggested scenarios for the future from among which the young people choose the one that seems to suit them. The structure of a milieu sets up guardrails that allow the young person to make his shift and feel initiated as a resilient person but without trauma.

When his development has made him vulnerable; when his family is in ruins on account of an illness, a serious conflict, or a disruptive immigration; when society no longer sets up guardrails or rituals allowing him to negotiate the shift, the adolescent may take a long time to assume his adult role. "The need for trauma is acute among the children of migrants . . . as a result of the parents' migratory logic."[185] Families shaken up, rites forgotten, adolescence prolonged: the young person is obliged to keep on functioning as a child even when he is eager to become an adult. By remaining passive, dependent on his early attachments, like a child he demands the immediate satisfaction of all his desires, including the sexual ones.

Because of the breakdown of familial and cultural structures, young people like this have not been able to use the sudden emergence of sexuality to leave their families and pursue another type of development. Deprived of tests and rites of separation or reparation, they are ashamed of still being in an infantile situation when they are already grown and intelligent and have earned degrees. All cultures have invented initiation rites that assist change and encourage autonomy, "for at these times neither the parents nor the cultural group can help [the young person] anticipate and bind anxiety."[186] As a rule, the "near trauma" of initiation rites offered by the culture is mitigated by the "cultural defenses" that cushion the shock and even turn it into a human advantage.[187] After the initiation the child has become more human, because he returns to the world of adults with a secret knowledge that makes a new man of him.

All cultures have invented initiation rites that take the form of ceremonies of passage: religious communions or welcoming newcomers to a business. Cultural guardrails usually prevent these welcoming ceremonies from being organized as sadistic hazing rituals, but when a young person has been traumatized or is unhappy in his family he tries to flee it for the adventure of early adolescence. He escapes, to be sure, but he has not completed his development. And so he finds himself thrust into a society that does not receive him well. It is in this group of premature adolescents who have not been able to establish a process of resilience that we find the greatest amount of risky sexual behavior. In this situation the risk becomes a dangerous initiation that can lead to destruction.

56. Emotional Security and Social Responsibility
Are the Primary Elements of Resilience

The mere fact of pursuing one's studies delays the first sexual encounter, makes for longer intervals between acts of intercourse, and reduces the number of partners and infidelities: "Those young men and women who leave school early escape the control of their family of origin sooner and are . . . led to begin their sex life without delay."[188]

This over-hasty social engagement is quite different from that of the young adultists who had to leave their parents very early on because they were beaten, insulted, or sexually assaulted. Like those who have moved on to social responsibilities, this latter group of adolescents rarely get involved in risky sex. Their social and emotional engagement does not at all conform to the current stereotype according to which a girl who has been raped will become a prostitute, an abused boy a sadist. On the contrary, such young people often form a very young, stable couple with an early parenthood that makes them responsible and thus testifies to the importance they attach to the family they dreamed of becoming. This early commitment got in the way of their studies but did not promote risky sex.

As soon as Jean turned 15 he left home to escape his violent and incestuous father. At 18 he bought a small hotel near a winter-sports resort and then went to get his 16-year-old sister. The two kids fixed up the hotel, working hard at the cooking and serving. They each chose to marry early, had children, and today lead picture-perfect lives. Their dreadful childhood remains painful, but their social and emotional success has made it possible for them to avoid tragic choices: staying in their family of origin with all its abuses, or rushing into an impulsive sociability without long-term plans.

Most young people with avoidant attachments come late to sexuality. They stay attached and faithful to partners they don't love, and eventually their distant emotional style slowly warms up.

It is not unusual for girls with ambivalent attachment to feel intense sexual desires at puberty that make them anxious. They stop grooming themselves and dress in baggy sweaters or blouses so that their breasts will not attract attention from boys. As for the teenagers tortured by strong desires they don't know how to express, they "turn these into their opposite,"[189] making vows of chastity or studying too hard so as to repress their sexual drives. The boys (more active, inhibited, or delinquent) and girls (more verbal, privacy-seeking, and depressive)[190] then begin a relational life in which they work to realize the opposite of their desires, undertaking a career of morbid sublimation that allows them to avoid the risk of sex.

In the group of adolescents with unbridled sexuality we find various forms of attachment. Some who have been too well behaved as children feel a sudden sense of freedom when they rush into risky sex. We find some inhibited children who are astonished by the revelation of sexuality and some young people who, after curbing their desires, suddenly abandon themselves to release. But most of these young people are those whose attachment was never formed. And so, when the drive sets in, they throw themselves into dangerous encounters; the first intercourse occurs around their twelfth year. At age 18, when other young people in the general population begin sexual relations, they have already had six or eight partners without using protection. In Quebec, 22 percent of the girls and 10 percent of the boys of this age have even had partners at high risk for AIDS.[191] In contrast to the advertising images of sensible young women teaching their male partners to use protection, 80 percent of these girls never use it, expecting the boy to take the initiative. Early pregnancy and sexually transmitted diseases amount to Russian roulette, a gamble with sexual risk and death.

Whether we are dealing with a teenager who does not know his own worth because he has been overprotected, too controlled by adults who made decisions for him, or with one who doesn't know who he is because he has been isolated and numbed in a formless environment, drugs offer a sense of personalization. The existential void is suddenly filled by sex acts, early pregnancies, and addiction, all of which finally, like a passion, provide a life project.[192]

Thus, while we cannot say that a troubled attachment leads to drugs or irresponsible sex, we can state that a serene attachment almost never does. When a young person has a life plan in which sexuality plays an important role, he doesn't have to go onstage and become the hero of a sordid tragedy. When these adolescents have no structure the theatricality of drugs helps them form a self-representation: "Finally something is happening to me. I've found drugs. I know how to get money. I have a lot of sexual encounters. I'm finally becoming someone in my own right." In the existential void as in the overabundance of emotion, nothing happens, and no self-representation can be constructed. Any event will do: illness that gives meaning and finally creates relationships, games of chance that erotize the risk of loss, competitive games in which the teenager can test his mettle, simulations of barbaric rituals, or dizzying games like parachute jumping or rock climbing in which the risk of falling creates a feeling of living through an extraordinary event.[193]

Conclusion

Up to the present time the problem has been simple, since it was
thought that each stroke of fate corresponded to an injury that could
be evaluated.

The advantage of simple problems is that they give observers the
impression of understanding. The inconvenience of simple problems
is that they make us forget that a stroke of fate is above all a mental
event. This is why we have to distinguish between the blow that comes
in the real world and the representation of this blow as elaborated in
the psychological world. The most damaging blows aren't always the
most spectacular ones. And the way we picture the blow in our internal world is a co-production of the private story the injured person
tells himself and the account given by his culture. The walking
wounded tell themselves what happened to them in order to get hold
of their shaken personality once again, whereas the witness prefers to
make use of archives and prejudices.

By the end of his life, one person in two will have experienced an
event that may be described as a trauma, an act of violence pushing
him close to death. One person in four will have had to face several
damaging events. One in ten will be unable to get rid of his psychological trauma. This amounts to saying that the others, by struggling
and engaging, will have succeeded in mending their torn personality
and returning to their place in the human adventure.[194]

This dynamic aspect of trauma explains the variability in the statistical accounts of resilience. Emergency units intervening after an attack
or catastrophe indicate that 20 percent of the people affected suffer from
trauma. But clinical descriptions and epidemiological studies are much
too static. They are true the way snapshots are true, ignoring "the way
symptoms can evolve, and . . . it is because of this static conception that
we have had to invent the notion of resilience."[195] What happens when
we escape trauma? What proportion of the wounded will be revisited
by the horror we thought they had overcome? These questions call for
studies covering the entire life cycle.

But they have all been dead, even those who returned home smiling. They have all been in the arms of the unnameable aggressor: death itself "in person."[196] We can go on living afterwards, even laugh about it when we come back from hell, but we hardly dare to admit that we feel initiated by the terrible experience. When we have lived among the dead, when we have lived through death, how can we say that we are ghosts? How can we make others understand that suffering is not depression, and that often the return to life is what hurts?

At a time when little thought was given to the process of resilience it was possible to state that "children who were abandoned or bereaved early on are three times more likely to suffer from depression as adults than the general population."[197] But ever since we have been helping to bring these children back to life, the number of cases of depression is exactly the same as in any human group.[198]

To hear the testimonies of the survivors, all we have to do is let them speak: Gilgamesh the Sumerian; Sisyphus, king of Corinth; and Orpheus of Thrace descended into hell. Achilles had already expressed the feeling of having been dead. The Napoleonic armies furnished a great many ghosts, like Colonel Chabert, made famous by Balzac. Dostoyevsky spoke of the indelible trace left in his memory by "the imprint of the house of the dead" in the Siberian penal colony.[199] But it is the twentieth century that has produced the greatest number of ghosts: the War of 1914–1918 described by Roland Dorgelès in *The Garden of the Dead*, Henri Barbusse in *Fire*, and Hermann Hesse in *Steppenwolf* told us how deeply ghosts invade life.

The hell of all hells was built with wooden huts in the Nazi extermination camps. Robert Antelme, banished from the human race,[200] and Primo Levi, who was considered a mere fragment, annulled as a human being by an avoidance of eye contact that made him as transparent as a shadow, had to mourn for themselves and become corpses among corpses. Jorge Semprun tried to be silent, to undergo "a long treatment of aphasia in order to survive."[201] Denial protected him by freezing part of his world until reality brought him back to full awareness when he saw newsreels showing the "private images" of piles of corpses in the Nazi camps. "We hadn't survived death. . . . We experienced it. . . . We are not survivors but ghosts."

There are cultures in which resilience is unthinkable; the organization of society has made it impossible. How are you supposed to become human again, when you are not allowed to learn your "job as a man"[202] because an accident has ripped apart the image under which you used to appear?

But when, despite the suffering, a desire is whispered, if only one other person hears it, the ember can burst into flame again.

> And on the brink of death
> At the ember's last moment
> The guitar enters the room
> Its dark song rekindles the fire.[203]

"My father was going to come back. . . . My mother promised me that when he did, everything would be better. She made him into a wonderful ghost—the most kind, handsome, strong, tender, best of fathers, and he was going to come back."[204]

It is not crazy to want to live, to hear at the bottom of the abyss a light breath whispering that, like an unthinkable sun, happiness awaits us.

Notes

1. J. Charyn (2000). Sugar Cane et la Princesse Rita. *Revue des Deux Mondes* July–August, p. 17.

2. J. Luquet (1996). *Hans Christian Andersen (1805–1875)*. Société française de psychologie adlérienne, *Bulletin* 85, p. 3. The following quotations are from p. 4 and p. 20, respectively. Here and in what follows, all translations from French sources are by S. F.

3. Resilience is a process that allows for the resumption of some kind of development despite trauma or adverse circumstances.

4. S. Vanistendael and J. Leconte (2000). *Le Bonheur est toujours possible*. Paris: Bayard.

5. Charles Dickens followed exactly the same course. Starting out as a child wounded by his father's imprisonment, which led to his family's extreme poverty, little Charles had to work from the age of 12 in a polishing factory. He was able to repair himself psychologically by telling stories. Later, in adulthood, he gave them up in favor of writing educational novels and engaging in social activities. See P. Ackroyd (1999). *Dickens*. London: Vintage.

6. C. Leroy discusses Alphonse Boudard and people suffering from sensory deprivation in G. DiGennaro, ed. (1975). *Space in the Prison*. London: Architectural Press.

7. A. Boudard (1963). *La Crise*. Paris: Plon.

8. D. Bisson and E. de Schonen (1993). *L'Enfant derrière la porte*, p. 10. Paris: Grasset.

9. Bisson and de Schonen (note 3), p. 27.

10. S. Freud (1895). Project for a scientific psychology. *Standard Edition* 1:281–397.

11. M. Leclercq-Olive (1997). *Le Dire de l'événement*. Villeneuve d'Ascq: Presses Universitaires de Septentrion.

12. M. Bertrand (2002). La Notion de traumatisme et ses avatars. *Le Journal des psychologues* 194, February.

13. J.Waldner (1995). Le Placement en institution. In J.-P. Pourtois, ed., *Blessure d'enfant*. Brussels: De Boeck University.

14. S. Freud (1917). Mourning and melancholia. *Standard Edition* 14:237–259.

15. J. Wier, cited in E. Pewsner (1992). *L'Homme coupable. La Folie et la faute en Occident*, p. 57. Paris: Privat.

16. L. Freden (1982). *Aspects psychosociaux de la dépression*. Sprimont: Pierre Mardaga.

17. E. M. Kranzler (1992). Early childhood bereavement. *Journal of the American Academy of Child and Adolescent Psychiatry* 29:513–520.

18. M. D. S. Ainsworth, M. C. Blehar, E. Waters, and S. Wall (1978). *Patterns of Attachment: A Psychological Study of the Strange Situation*. Hillsdale, NJ: Lawrence Erlbaum. Between the ages of 12 and 18 months, children in all groups in a standardized observation situation manifest an attachment profile in which:

> —65 percent have attained secure attachment: they like to explore because they feel loved;
> —20 percent have attained ambivalent attachment: they attack those they love;
> —15 percent struggle against their feelings in order to suffer less;
> —5 percent are confused.

The total is greater than 100 percent because of the instability of insecure attachments.

19. M. Hanus (2001). *La Résilience, à quel prix?*, p. 62. Paris: Maloine.

20. M. Berger (2002). L'Utilité des critères indicateurs de placements? *Journal du droit des jeunes* 213:18–23.

21. Berger (note 20).

22. F. Mohout (2001). Le devenir des enfants de l'Aide social à l'enfance. *Devenir* 13:31–66.

23. S. Ionescu and C. Jourdan-Ionescu (2001). La résilience des enfants roumains abandonnés, institutionnalises et infectés par le virus du sida. In M. Manciaux, ed., *La Résilience. Résister et se construire*, pp. 95–99. Geneva: Médicine et Hygiène.

24. T. G. O'Connor, D. Bredenkamp, and M. Rutter (1999). Attachment disturbances and disorders in children exposed to early severe deprivation. *Infant Mental Health Journal* 20:10–29.

25. A. Clarke (2000). *Early Experience and the Life Path.* London: Kingsley.

26. Lecompte (2002). *Briser le cycle de la violence. Quand d'anciens enfants maltraités deviennent des parents non maltraitants.* Doctoral thesis in psychology, Toulouse, Ecole pratique des hautes études.

27. D. B. Bugenta (1993). Communication in abusive relationships: cognitive constructions of interpersonal power. *America Behavioral Scientist* 36:288–308.

28. D. Ciccetti, S. Toth, and M. Bush (1998). Developmental psychopathology and competence in children: suggestions and interventions. In B. B. Lahey and A. E. Kazdin, eds., *Advances in Clinical Child Psychology*, vol. 11, pp. 1–77. New York: Plenum.

29. S.-L. Ethier (1999). *La Négligence et la violence envers les enfants.* Boucherville (Quebec): Gaétan Morin.

30. M. Emmanuelli (2001). Quotient intellectuel. *Dictionnaire de psychopathologie de l'enfant et de l'adolescent.* Paris: PUF.

31. A. Dumaret and J. Stewart (1989). Récupération des retards du développement psychologique après disparition des facteurs environnementaux néfastes. *La Psychiatrie d'enfant* 32:593–615.

32. A. Tabouret-Keller (1999). Thomas Platter, a wandering scholar at the beginning of the sixteenth century. *Le Furet* 30:50–53.

33. C. G. Banaag (1997). *Resiliency: Stories Found in Philippine Streets.* UNICEF.

34. E. Leroy-Ladurie (1995). *Le Siècle de Platter, 1499–1628*, vol. 1, pp. 41–42. Paris: Fayard.

35. Leroy-Ladurie (note 34), p. 42.

36. See Banaag (note 33), p. 5. There are 120 million street children on the planet today, according to Dominique Versini (UNESCO, November 21, 2002).

37. A. Berrada (2002). *Migration et sécurité de l'enfant. Droits de l'enfant et sécurité humaine dans l'espace euro-méditerranéen.* Paper delivered in Marrakech, October. Hervé Le Bras, on the other hand, believes that populations will stick to their places of origin.

38. This does not happen in traumatic syndromes in which the wound keeps on bleeding as though it had just occurred.

39. F. Cano, M. E. Colmenares, A. C. Delgado, and M. E. Villalobos (2002). *La Resiliencia. Responsabilidad del sujeto y esperanza social.* Colombia: Rafue.

40. R. Fivush (1998). Children's recollections of traumatic and non-traumatic events. *Development and Psychopathology* 10:699–716.

41. S. Ferenczi (1932). The confusion of tongues between adults and children: the language of tenderness and passion. In M. Balint, ed., *Final Contributions to the Problems and Methods of Psychoanalysis*, trans. E. Mosbacher, pp. 156–167. London: Karnac, 1980.

42. R. Puyelo (1999). L'Odyssée psychanalytique. In A. Konichekis, J. Forest, and R. Puyelo, eds., *Narration et psychanalyse*, pp. 139–140. Paris: L'Harmattan.

43. G. Bonnet (1999). Narration et narcissisation. In Konichekis et al. (note 42 above), pp. 38–40.

44. D. Cicchetti and B. Nurcombe, eds. (1998). Risk, trauma, and memory. *Development and Psychopathology* 10.4. Cambridge, UK: Cambridge University Press.

45. M. E. Pipe, J. Dean, J. Canning, and T. Murachuer (1996). Narrating events and telling stories. Paper delivered at the Conference on Memory. Albano, July.

46. A. Houbbalah (1998). *Destin du traumatisme*. Paris: Hachette.

47. R. Fivush (1993). Developmental perspectives on autobiographical recall. In G. S. Goodman and B. L. Bottoms, eds., *Child Victims, Child Witnesses*. New York: Guilford.

48. J.-L. Viaux (1995). Expertise d'enfant, parole de victime, fonction du juridique. In M. Gabel, S. Lebovici, P. Mazet, and J.-L. Viaux, eds., *Le Traumatisme de l'inceste*. Paris: PUF.

49. P. Bensussan (2002). Témoignage négligé, allégation abusive. *Sexologos*, January.

50. M.-D. Vergez and M. De Maximy (1999). Regards juridiques croisés dans un cas d'allégation d'abus sexuel. In M. Manciaux and D. Girodet, eds., *Allégation d'abus sexuel. Paroles d'enfant, paroles d'adultes*, pp. 129–143. Paris: Fleurus.

51. P. Parseval and G. Delaisi de Parseval (2000). Les pères qui divorcent seraient-ils tous des abuseurs sexuels? *Journal du Droit des Jeunes*, June.

52. P. Ariès and G. Duby (1985). *Histoire de la vie privée*, vol. 3, p. 319. Paris: Seuil.

53. Aries and Duby (note 52 above), p. 323.

54. A. Miller (1984). *C'est pour ton bien. Racines de la violence dans l'éducation de l'enfant*. Paris: Aubier.

55. B. Pierrehumbert (2001). *Attachement et systèmes familiaux*. Thesis, University of Toulon, November.

56. A. F. Newcomb, W. M. Bukowski, and L. Patte (1993). A meta-analytic review of popular, rejected, neglected, controversial, and average sociometric status. *Psychological Bulletin* 113:99–128.

57. V. Lew and M. Boily (1999). *Les Risques psychosociaux chez les enfants de personnes atteintes de maladie mentale*. Boucherville (Quebec): Gaétan Moran.

58. J. Lecamus (2001). *Le Vrai rôle du père*. Paris: Odile Jacob.

59. M. Ravoisin, J.-P. Pourtois, and H. Desmet (2000). Les enfants d'ouvrier en Polytechnique. In J.-P. Pourtois and H. Desmet, eds., *Relations familiales et résilience*, pp. 173–195. Paris: L'Harmattan.

60. G. Charpak and D. Saudinois (1993). *La Vie à fil tendu*. Paris: Odile Jacob.

61. P. Nimal, W. Lahaye, and J.-P. Pourtois (2001). *Trajectoires familiales d'insertion sociale*. Brussels: De Boeck.

62. C. Enjolet (1997). *Princesse d'ailleurs*. Paris: Phébus.

63. See Banaag (note 33 above).

64. Y. Le Menn and M. Le Bris (1995). *Fragments du royaume*. Grigny: Parole d'Aube.

65. W. Golding (1954). *Lord of the Flies*. New York: Perigee.

66. J. Dryden, B. R. Johnson, S. Howard, and A. McGuire (1998). Resiliency: A comparison arising from conversations with 9–12-year-old children and their teachers. Paper presented at the annual meeting of the American Educational Research Association. San Diego, April.

67. J.-L. Bauvois and R. V. Joule (1998). La psychologie de la soumission. *La Recherche* 202:1050–1057.

68. S. Bellil (2002). *Dans l'enfer des tournantes*. Paris: Denoël.

69. M. Gannage (1999). *L'Enfant, les parents, et la guerre*. Paris: ESF.

70. D. Schwatrz, R. Stevens, N. McFadden-Ketchun, et al. (1998). Peer group victimisation as a predictor of children's behavior problems at home and at school. *Development and Psychopathology*. Cambridge, UK: Cambridge University Press.

71. J. R. Meloy (1992). *Violent Attachment*. Northvale, NJ: Jason Aronson.

72. E. Debarbieux and C. Blaya (2001). *La Violence en milieu scolaire*. Paris: ESF.

73. R. Myrick (1997). *Developmental Guidance and Counseling: A Practical Approach*. Minneapolis: Educational Medical Corporation.

74. E. U. Hodges and D. G. Perry (1995). *Behavioral and Social Antecedents and Consequences of Victimization by Peers*. Indianapolis: Society for Research in Child Development.

75. E. Werner and R. Smith (1988). *Vulnerable but Invincible: A Longitudinal Study of Resilient Children and Youth*. New York: Adams, Bannister, & Cox.

76. A. Hicklin (2002). The warrior class. *The Independent*, February 21.

77. A. Vasquez-Bronfman and J. Martinez (1996). *La Socialisation à l'école*. Paris: PUF.

78. M. Ravoisin, J.-P. Pourtois, and H. Desmet (note 59 above).

79. Centre de recherche et d'innovation en sociopédagogie familiale et scolaire (CERIS), University of Mons-Hainaut.

80. J. Miermont (2001). Parentification. *Dictionnaire des thérapies familiales*. Paris: Payot.

81. G. Harrus-Redivi (2001). *Parents immatures et enfants-adultes*, p. 14. Paris: Payot.

82. S. Ferenczi (note 41).

83. J. Barudy (1997). *La Douleur invisible de l'enfant*. Ramonville-Saint-Ange: Erès.

84. M. Foucault (1963). *The Birth of the Clinic*. New York: Vintage, 1994.

85. A. Oppenheimer (1994). Enfant, enfance, infantile. *Revue française de psychanalyse*.

86. M. Coppel-Batsch (1999). Georges Perec, romancier de la psychanalyse. *Les Temps modernes* 604:199.

87. G. Perec (1975). *W, ou le souvennir d'enfance*. Paris: Denoël.

88. J. Bruner (1991). *Car la culture donne forme à l'esprit*. Paris: Eshel.

89. Bruner (note 88 above), p. 58.

90. N. de Saint-Phalle (1994). *Mon secret*, p. 5. Paris: La Différence.

91. S. Freud, quoted in J. Laplanche and J.-B. Pontalis (1967). *Idéal de moi*, p. 184. Paris: PUF.

92. A. Freud (1936). *The Ego and the Mechanisms of Defense*. New York: International Universities Press.

93. M. Bellet (2001). *Les Survivants*. Paris: L'Harmattan.

94. A. de Cacqueray and J. Dieudonné (2000). Familles d'écrivains. *Archives et culture*.

95. S. Freud (1954). *The Origins of Psychoanalysis. Letters to Wilhelm Fliess*. New York: Basic Books.

96. S. Ionescu, M.-M. Jacquet, and C. Lothe (1997). *Les Mécanismes de défense*, p. 253. Paris: Nathan.

97. J.-P. Klein and E. Viarm (2001). L'art, exploration de l'intime. *Cultures en mouvements* 34.

98. F. Hölderlin (1797). *Hypérion*, p. 21. Paris: Gallimard, 1973.

99. J. Russ (1998). *Le Tragique créateur*. Paris: Armand Colin.

100. C. Masson (2001). *L'Angoisse et la création*. Paris: L'Harmattan.

101. G. Perec (note 87 above).

102. N. de Saint-Phalle (note 90 above).

103. N. Abraham and M. Torok (1987). *L'Ecorce et le noyau*. Paris: Flammarion.

104. F. Ponge (1948). *Le Parti pris des choses*. Paris: Gallimard.

105. C. Masson (note 100 above), p. 154.

106. M. Proust (1927). *Remembrance of Things Past*, vol. 6: *Time Regained*, trans. C. K. Scott Moncrieff. New York: Penguin, 1999.

107. F. Lignon (1998). *Erich von Stroheim. Du ghetto au gotha*. Paris: L'Harmattan.

108. P. Ackroyd (1991). *Dickens*. New York: HarperCollins.

109. G. Gusdorf (1990). *L'Ecriture du moi*, vol. 2, p. 200. Paris: Odile Jacob.

110. P. Aries and G. Duby (note 53), p. 158.

111. C. Perrault (1697). *Vieux contes françaises*. Paris: Flammarion, 1980.

112. H. Malot (1878). *Sans famille*. Paris: Hachette, 1933.

113. Cited in A. Gianfrancesco (2001). *Une littérature de résilience?*, p. 27. Geneva: Médicine et Hygiène. See also E. Charton (1981). *Mendier. Enfance et éducation d'un paysan au XVIIIe siècle*. Paris: Le Sycomore.

114. R. Shafer (1976). *A New Language for Psychoanalysis*. New Haven, CT: Yale University Press.

115. M. Rustin (1991). *The Good Society and the Inner World*. New York: Vintage.

116. A. Solzhenitsyn (1974). *The Gulag Archipelago*. New York: Perennial, 2002.

117. G. Pineau and J.-L. Legrand (2000). *Les Histoires de vie*. Paris: PUF.

118. M. Myquel (2001). Mythomanie. *Dictionnaire de psychopathologie de l'enfant*. Paris: PUF.

119. J. Semprun (1972). *Le grand voyage*. Paris: Gallimard.

120. S. Smith (2002). *J. K. Rowling*. Lausanne: Favre.

121. F. Uhlman (1997). *L'Ami retrouvé*. Paris: Gallimard.

122. J.-P. Gueno (1998). *Paroles des poilus. Lettres et carnets du front, 1914–1918*, pp. 104–105. Paris: Librio.

123. E. Carrère (2000). *L'Adversaire*. Paris: POL.

124. P. Romon (2002). *Le bienfaiteur*. Paris: L'Archipel.

125. P. Romon (note 124), p. 167.

126. S. Vanistendael (2002). *La Spiritualité*. Geneva: Bureau International Catholique de l'Enfance.

127. E. Carrère (note 123 above), pp. 183–184.

128. F. Lignon (note 107 above), p. 9.

129. F. Lignon (note 107 above), p. 27; cf. p. 324.

130. E. Lappin (1999). *L'Homme qui avait deux têtes*. Paris: L'Olivier.

131. G. Maurey (1996). *Mentir. Bienfaits et méfaits*, p. 123. Brussels: De Boeck.

132. E. J. Menvielle (1996). *Psychiatric Outcome and Psychosocial Intervention for Children Exposed to Trauma*. Geneva: International Catholic Child Bureau.

133. For the past several decades there has been a taboo on the word *normal*. Yet there are three possible definitions of the norm:

1. The statistical norm or "average."
2. The normative norm of a culture.
3. The evaluative norm referring to a person's optimal functioning.

See D. Houzel (2000). Normal et pathologique. In D. Houzel, M. Emmanuelli, and F. Moggio, eds., *Dictionnaire de psychopathologie de l'enfant et de l'adolescent*, p. 457. Paris: PUF.

134. E. La Maisonneuve (1997). *La Violence qui vient*. Paris: Arlea.

135. The Mozambiquan Public Health Association.

136. Doctoral thesis in psychology, cited in J. Kreisler (1996). Enfants-soldats au Mozambique. *Enfance majuscule* 31:4.

137. Kreisler (note 136 above), p. 24.

138. M. Grappe (2002). *Le devenir des jeunes combattants*. Paper read at the Scientific Research Group of CERI, B. De Poligny. Paris, March 7.

139. M. Grappe (note 138 above).

140. S. Tomkiewicz (1996). L'Enfant et la guerre. *Enfance majuscule* 31:13.

141. G. Mootoo (2000). *Sierra Leone. Une enfance perdue.* Amnesty International.

142. J. Vicari (1999). Résilience, urbanisme, et lieux de rencontre. In M.-P. Poltot, ed., *Souffrir mais se construire.* Paris: Eres.

143. S. Roché (2002). Délinquances des jeunes. *Sciences humaines* 129. See also S. Roché (2002). *Tolérance zéro.* Paris: Odile Jacob.

144. L. Bègue (2002). Sentiment d'injustice et délinquance. *Futurible* 274.

145. Personal communication from Mrs. Bruère-Dawson.

146. M. Vaillant (2000). L'hypothèse transitionnelle dans la réparation. *Journal du droit des jeunes* 196.

147. P. Dubéchot and P. Le Queau (1998). Quartiers prioritaires. Les jeunes qui "s'en sortent." *Consommation et modes de vie* 126.

148. J.-F. Mattei, personal communication, September 2002.

149. Robert Clément, dir. (1946).

150. W. Staudte, dir. (1946). *Die Mörder sind unter uns.*

151. P. Centlivres, D. Fabre, and F. Zonabend, eds. (1998). *La Fabrique des héros.* Paris: Maison des sciences de l'homme.

152. Everyone, that is, who has not gone to the Louvre to see De Weerts's picture of a big boy with white skin who is placed in front of a splendid white horse that is rearing up and is about to be impaled on the pitchforks of the grimacing people of the Vendée.

153. G. Droniou (2001). *Fesch, mon nom guillotiné*, p. 40. Paris: Editions du Rocher.

154. Droniou (note 154 above), p. 65.

155. Droniou (note 154 above), p. 168.

156. A. Muxel (1998). Le héros des jeunes Français: vers un humanisme politique réconciliateur. In P. Centlivres et al. (note 151 above), pp. 80–81.

157. Muxel (note 156 above), p. 86.

158. L. A. Sroufe (1996). *Emotional Development: The Organization of Emotional Life in the Early Years.* Cambridge, UK: Cambridge University Press.

159. E. Palacio-Quintin (2000). Les relations d'attachements multiples de l'enfant comme élément de résilience. In Pourtois and Desmet (Part I, note 59 above), p. 119.

160. F. A. Goosens and M. H. van Ijzendoorn (1990). Quality of an infant's attachment to professional caregivers. *Child Development* 61:832–837.

161. R. A. Thomson (1991). *Construction and Reconstruction of Early Attachment.* Hillsdale, NJ: Lawrence Erlbaum.

162. C. Rodhain (1986). *Le Destin bousculé.* Paris: Robert Laffont.

163. T. Masao (1999). *Homo japonicus.* Paris: Picquier. I am grateful to Muriel Jolivet for this reference.

164. C. Chalot (1980). La croyance en un monde juste comme variable intermédiare de réaction au sort d'autrui et à son propre sort. *Psychologie française* 25:1.

165. Lappin (note 130 above), p. 15.

166. R. Robin (2000). La judiciarisation de l'holocauste. *La Lettre des amis de la CCE* 29:14.

167. G. Lopez and A. Casanova (2001). *Il n'est jamais trop tard pour cesser d'être une victime*, p. 88. Brussels: EDLM.

168. Ségolène Royal, the Minister of the Family, made this a program of social action starting in 2000.

169. L. S. Ethier (1999). La négligence et la violence envers les enfants. *Psychopathologie de l'enfant et de l'adolescent: approche intégrative*, p. 604. Boucherville (Quebec): Gaëtan Morin.

170. M. Erickson and B. Egeland (1996). Child neglect. In J. Brière, L. Berliner, J. Buckley, and C. Jenny, eds., *Handbook of Child Maltreatment*, pp. 4–20. New York: Sage.

171. P. K. Trickette and C. McBride-Chang (1995). The developmental impact of different forms of child abuse and neglect. *Developmental Review* 15:311–337.

172. C. Hazan and C. Shaver (1994). Attachment as an organizational framework for research on close relationships. *Psychological Inquiry* 5:122.

173. A. Duperey (2002). *Allons plus loin, veux-tu?* Paris: Seuil.

174. M. J. Paulson, D. Stone, and R. Sposto (1978). Suicide potential and behavior in children ages 4 to 12. *Threatening Behavior* 8:225–242.

175. S. M. Consoli (2000). Du stress à la souffrance physique. *Revue française de psychiatrie et de psychologie médicale* 4.38.

176. B. Golse (2001). L'attachement à l'adolescence. *L'Autre* 2:109–116.

177. E. Waters, S. Merrick, D. Reboux, L. L. J. Crowell, and L. Albersheim

(2000). Attachment security in infancy and early adulthood. *Twenty-Year Longitudinal Study* 71:684–689.

178. Y. Mukagasana (1998). *Ils ont tué mes enfants*. Paris: Fixot.

179. S. Tomkiewicz (1996). L'enfant et la guerre. *Enfance majuscule* 31.

180. E. Mueller and N. Silverman (1989). Peer relations in maltreated children. In D. Cicchetti and V. Carlson, eds., *Child Maltreatment. Theory and Research on the Course and Consequences of Child Abuse and Neglect*, pp. 529–578. Cambridge, UK: Cambridge University Press.

181. Enjolet (note 62), p. 129. The following citation is from p. 56.

182. The variation in numbers from one study to another depends on where and how the information was collected, but the order of magnitude remains the same.

183. D. Pleux (2002). *De l'enfant roi à l'enfant tyran*. Paris: Odile Jacob.

184. M. R. Moro (2002). *Enfants d'ici venus d'ailleurs*, p. 102. Paris: La Découverte.

185. Moro (note 184 above), p. 102.

186. Moro (note 184 above), p. 103.

187. G. Devereux (1967). *De l'angoisse à la méthode*. Paris: Flammarion, 1980.

188. M. Bozon and H. Léridon (1993). *Sexualité et sciences sociales*, p. 1334. Paris: Ined/PUF.

189. S. Ionescu, M.-M. Jacquet, and C. Lothe (1997). *Les Mécanismes de défense. Théorie et clinique*, p. 263. Paris: Nathan.

190. J. E. Fleming and D. R. Offord (1990). Epidemiology of childhood depressive disorders. *Journal of the American Academy of Child and Adolescent Psychiatry* 29:571–586.

191. J.-Y. Frappier, C. Roy, D. A. Morin, and D. H. Morin (1997). *L'infection d'VIH chez les adolescents en difficulté de Montréal*. Personal communication.

192. M. Lejoyeux, M. Claudon, and J. Mourad (1999). La dépendance alcoolique: données clinique et psychopathologiques. *Perspectives psy* 38.

193. R. Caillois (1960). *Les Jeux et les hommes*. Paris: Gallimard.

194. R. Yehuda (1997). Le DST prédicteur du PTSD. *Abstract Neuro-psy* 168:10.

195. M. Bertrand (2002). La notion du traumatisme et ses avatars. *Le Journal des psychologues* 194:22.

196. C. Barrois (1995). Traumatisme et inceste. In M. Gabel, S. Lebovici, and P. Mazet, eds., *Le Traumatisme de l'inceste*, p. 19. Paris: PUF.

197. M. Toussignant (1992). *Les Origines sociales et culturelles des troubles psychologiques*, p. 122. Paris: PUF.

198. C. Sabatier (1999). La culture, l'immigration et la santé mentale des enfants. *Psychopathologie de l'enfant et de l'adolescent*, p. 551. Boucherville (Quebec): Gaetan Morin.

199. L. Crocq (2000). Le retour des enfers et son message. *Revue francophone du stress et du trauma* 1:5–19.

200. R. Antelme (1957). *L'Espèce humaine*. Paris: Gallimard.

201. J. Semprun (1994). *L'Ecriture ou la vie*. Paris: Gallimard.

202. A. Jollien (2002). *Le Métier de l'homme*. Paris: Seuil.

203. L. Aragon (1963). *Le Fou d'Elsa*, p. 417. Paris: Gallimard.

204. J. P. Gueno (2002). *Paroles d'étoiles*, p. 135. Paris: France-bleu.